THE STEPHANIE

Like rose dreams and shadow lights

The beauty of The Stephanie

Lies in her repose.

Intriguing as the Greek goddess Aphrodite

She appears to have sprung

Fully formed from the sea,

A lovely maiden

An exquisite shell

Pressed to the sand

Sunlit, fire warmed

A glowing fog star

Of the Oregon Coast.

No stranger,

Past and present

Merge in her sunset glance

Graceful observer

To puffin whimsy

And Haystack tradition.

Her serene scallop half smile

The Stephanie waiting

Sweet poetry

To all who discover her.

Composed in honor of the opening of The Stephanie Inn

by Laura Drumheller

April 1993

THE Stephanie Inn
COOKBOOK

Lori McKean

WITH

Chef John Newman

acknowledgements

First and foremost, thanks to the women of The Stephanie Inn: Jan Martin, Stephanie Snyder, and Jennifer Booth for helping to create one of the world's most inviting and romantic inns. A special tribute is due to the late Steve Martin, for his vision and his passion for hospitality. Many thanks are also due to Ryan Snyder and Bill Booth.

Special thanks go to Stephanie Inn Manager, Sharon Major, and her staff. Thanks also to Executive Chef, John Newman, for his talent and passion, and to his dining room staff, Sharon Wucherpfennig, Lois Roberts, Crystal Davis, Joel Francis, Gehrett Billinger, Aristeo Maldonado, Will Leroux, and Wes McMillen.

Thanks also to Bill Canessa, Abbie Hart, Judy Lindsey, Ron Logan, Dave Norstedt, and Tamara Roberts, to Valerie Ryan and The Cannon Beach Book Company, Machele Brass and Brass Design, Jim Kingwell and Suzanne Kindland from Icefire Glassworks in Cannon Beach, Sherrie Meier, and Masato Yoshino.

Bon Appetit to everyone not mentioned above who assisted with recipe testing/tasting: Stephen Snyder and Emma Hart (who at a very young age taste-tested their first recipes), Mary and Roger Friesen, Jean Oberem, Mike Cushman, Gene and Gloria Logan, Tari and Casey Corkrey, Kim Logan, Ben Christianson, Paul Tice and Kim Christianson, Charlie Rehwalt, Jennifer Smieja and Mark Gustavson, for letting us experiment.

Thank you to photographer John Rizzo for the incredible images. And, thanks to our designer, Linda Wisner, for pulling this all together and making it beautiful.

In addition to those mentioned above, Executive Chef John Newman thanks his wonderful, supportive wife, Sandy Newman, his loving mother, Sesame Smith, and his Lord and Savior, Jesus Christ.

Author, Lori McKean, thanks EVERYONE mentioned above, along with her parents, Janet and Bill Davis, her sister, Linda Armstrong, and her English Mastiff, Kuma, for their ongoing love and support.

Food and Inn photography by John A. Rizzo, Portland Oregon.
Historic photography courtesy of the Cannon Beach Historical Society
Design by Linda Wisner, Wisner Creative, Portland, Oregon
Photo styling by Lori McKean and John Newman

ISBN 0-9749227-0-6

The Stephanie Poem

WELCOME TO THE STEPHANIE INN

When The Stephanie Inn in Cannon Beach, Oregon, first opened its doors to the public in 1993, the visions and dreams of many people had come true, most importantly, those of Steve and Jan Martin, and their daughter, Stephanie Snyder. This cookbook, based on the delicious recipes prepared and served to the Inn's guests, is another dream realized. Neither the Inn nor this cookbook could have happened without the vision of some incredible people. The remarkable history and romance of the small coastal town of Cannon Beach played an important role, as well.

Perched on the edge of the majestic Pacific Ocean in Cannon Beach, The Stephanie Inn offers magnificent views of the world-famous basalt monolith Haystack Rock to the north, and its sister, Silver Point Rock, to the south. Open the doors to your balcony, and you are at the ocean. The rhythmic roar of the sea is powerful yet peaceful, providing a symphony of water and foam, shifting sounds, and kaleidoscopic colors changing from aqua to white, to silver, slate, evergreen and pink. The ocean waves explode over the base of Haystack Rock, with foam spraying upwards of 20 feet high. Seagulls lift like kites over the water, then dive to the swells in search of food. Giant pelicans glide over the tops of waves in single file, filling the horizon with the grace of a Japanese watercolor.

Framed by Haystack Rock and Tillamook Head to the north, Silver Point to the south, the Pacific Ocean to the west, and the coastal mountains to the east, The Stephanie Inn is an oasis. There, visitors can enjoy the rugged beauty of Cannon Beach within the comfort and elegance of a world-class resort offering Northwest regional dining at its gourmet best.

A picnic from the chef, spread out in front of the Inn.

No wonder world travelers often meet others who recognize The Stephanie Inn and Cannon Beach. Former guests are often heard to say, "It is our favorite place to stay anywhere in the world." Visit the Inn and you'll soon understand why people feel this way. The Stephanie Inn is a sanctuary from the busy demands of everyday life, offering comfort, camaraderie, and unparalleled beauty. The gracious staff welcomes all guests with beaming smiles and exceptional customer service, a keynote to the Inn's success.

THE INN'S BEGINNINGS

For many years, founders and owners Jan and Steve Martin visited Cannon Beach as their favorite getaway. Deciding this was the place where they wanted to live and work, they moved to Cannon Beach in 1979 with their seven-year-old daughter, Stephanie. The Martins purchased their first hotel in the area, the Surfsand Resort, and followed that with the acquisition of other local properties, including the Haystack Resort, the Wayfarer Restaurant, R.V. Resort in Cannon Beach, and two properties in The Dalles, Oregon. The Viking Motel, a partnership with long-time

The Lobby

friend Bill Booth, is the site of The Stephanie Inn. Opened in April of 1993, The Stephanie Inn is a world-class resort property, renowned for its setting, service, and elegant dining.

It took ten years of research, visiting inns across the country with their daughter Stephanie and the manager of the Inn, Sharon Major, to identify the elegant yet comfortable ambience the Martins wanted for The Stephanie Inn. Their vision was to create an inn where people would feel as though they were guests in their own home. Working with local artist/designer Ray Watkins and designers Abbott Heys and Associates Architecture, they made their vision a reality.

Interiors built of recycled old-growth wood and fireplaces built from local stone add a touch of rustic elegance to the Inn. Furnishings include many special touches. There's a beautiful piano in the oceanfront library and wicker and wood furniture grace the rooms throughout. Majestic, cozy, and elegant at once, The Stephanie Inn offers the grace of one of Europe's finest hotels, balanced by the charm of a coastal country inn.

The Chart Room

the rooms at the inn

Barbara Sue • Jean Elizabeth •
Mary Bernadette • Kristin Rose •
Barbara Lucille • Lois May • Julie
Karen • Joanne Margaret • Mary
Jane • Carol Susan • Jane Adele •
Geraldine Luana • Kimberly Dawn •
Abigail Jane • Leona Velena • Katie
Lynn • Jennifer Anne • Alison •
Shirley Louise • Partricia Ann •
Anna Emelia • Janice Kay • Winifred
Sarann • Barbara Pearl •
Geraldine Loise • Cheri Jeanine •
Tracey Ann • Beth Ann • Cheryl
Ann • Cannie Barbara • Michelle
Denice • Della Faye • Barbara
Fettig • Irma Wilhelmina • Brook
Heather • Virginialee • Helen
Marie • Kathleen Ellen • Mercedes
Foley • Rhonda Jean • Gabriele
Christine • Shirley Isabel •
Lorraine Marie • Christy Linn •
Kimberly Anne • Britney Linn •
Carolee • Stephanie Nell • Sharon
Rose • Jennifer Teal •

Gracious Comforts

Stephanie Inn guests are treated to a complimentary wine and cheese gathering, held each evening in the library and chartroom overlooking the ocean and Haystack Rock. Guests gather around the fireplace or piano as they did at the town's inns in the 1800s and early 1900s to enjoy the ocean view and to talk with old and new friends. A jigsaw puzzle in the inviting entryway offers guests a chance to sit around a warm fire. Freshly baked cookies in the cookie jar at the front desk and coffee and tea are always available. New acquaintances at the Inn often join each other for dinner and even plan their next summer holiday together.

The Women of The Stephanie Inn

Each room at The Stephanie Inn is named for a special female family member or friend of the Martin or Booth families. Jan Martin refers to them as "noteworthy ladies." Of course, the Inn was named for daughter Stephanie. The "Jennifer Anne Suite", a two-bedroom corner suite on the second floor, is named for Jennifer Booth. And there is the "Janice Kay Room," named for Jan Martin, a very special room overlooking Haystack Rock and offering sweeping panoramic views of the coastline.

Recipes from the Women Owners of The Stephanie Inn

Each of the women owners of The Stephanie Inn was asked to contribute one of their favorite recipes to this book. Stephanie has a recipe for Barbeque Lime-Chicken Fajitas (page 108); Jan Martin's recipe is a Broccoli Casserole with Pimientos and Slivered Almonds (page 128); and Jennifer Booth offers a Lemon Cake Custard (page 144). While these are not dishes served in the Inn's dining room, they are delicious and welcome additions to this cookbook.

The Janice Kay Room

The Company Philosophy

The company philosophy is simple and it begins with a feeling of family, from the owners and employees to the guests. The result is that each person who stays at the Inn is treated as if they were personal guests in the Martin's home. Everything is done to ensure that their guest's stay is as comfortable as possible. "This has been a wonderful venture and a labor of love that has surpassed all of our expectations, and of which we are truly proud," says owner Jan Martin. "We hope that we have made each of our guest's lives a little better."

COOKING IN THE STEPHANIE INN KITCHEN

The kitchen at The Stephanie Inn comes alive early each morning, about 5:30 AM, when the breakfast chef arrives. Wonderful aromas fill the air as the chef mixes yeast, sugar, milk and salt—the starter for the Inn's fragrant, homemade bread. Fresh scones and muffins lend a sweet, buttery scent to tempt the taste buds. The kitchen begins to bustle with activity as cooks and staff arrive. The smell of dark roasted coffee swirls as eggs are scrambled, colorful fresh fruit is sliced, and bowls of hearty granola are set out to accompany one of the house specialties, such as Scotch Eggs or Buttermilk-Cheddar Cheese Biscuits with Sausage and Bacon Gravy. Soon, the breakfast guests begin to arrive, and there is a flurry of excitement as cooks keep the buffet filled with an array of freshly prepared foods.

At 10:30 AM, when the last guests have finished their breakfast, there is a wonderful lull. The Stephanie Inn staff gathers to enjoy the buffet and relax for a few minutes before it's time to return to the kitchen to pull freshly baked loaves of bread from the oven. They are replaced by sheets full of cookie dough so that the big cookie jar in the lobby can be replenished all day long. The finishing touches for the evening's dessert, such as spun sugar, or chocolate-dipped strawberries are completed just as the dinner chefs begin to arrive.

Making sauces, grilling vegetables, preparing garnishes, grilling meats and seafood and making salads for up to 80 people all takes place in the confines of a tiny kitchen where everyone works comfortably, side by side. Nightly menus feature the freshest, best quality foods the region has to offer, served in very innovative ways. One April menu featured a Butter Lettuce Salad with Avocado, Crispy Shallots, and Grapefruit Vinaigrette, followed by Curried Lentil Soup with Coriander-Lime Cream and Fried Taro Root. For entrées, guests might choose between Pan Seared Scallops with Jasmine Rice served with Zucchini and Caper Sauce or Stone-Ground Mustard Lamb Racks with Herbed Spatzle, Braised Greens and Wine Syrup—not an easy choice. Topping this particular menu was a gorgeous Dried Fruit Stuffed Apple with Caramel Sauce and Homemade Cinnamon Ice Cream. It is difficult to believe that all this happens in a small, intimate kitchen on the Oregon Coast.

The Dining Room

THE KITCHEN PHILOSOPHY

AT THE STEPHANIE INN, THE CHEF'S FOCUS IS BASED ON CLASSIC COOKING TECHNIQUES COMBINED WITH INNOVATIVE INGREDIENTS AND PRESENTATIONS. THE BASIC PREMISE OF GOOD COOKING IS TO START WITH THE FRESHEST, LOCAL SEASONAL INGREDIENTS THE CHEFS CAN FIND, SUCH AS PRODUCE FROM LOCAL FARMS; WILD MUSHROOMS, WILD WATERCRESS, SEA-BEANS, AND BERRIES FROM LOCAL FORAGERS; JUST CAUGHT FISH, CRAB, OR CLAMS, FROM LOCAL SHORES; AND EXCEPTIONAL LOCAL WINES AND CHEESES. THE GOAL IN COOKING IS TO LET THE FOOD SPEAK FOR ITSELF—DON'T OVER-MANIPULATE IT. WITH AN EMPHASIS ON SEASONINGS AND EXECUTION, THE CHEFS AT THE STEPHANIE INN DO EVERYTHING POSSIBLE TO HIGHLIGHT EACH FOOD'S NATURAL FLAVOR, COLOR, AND TEXTURE.

When following the recipes in this book, keep in mind that much cooking is based on improvisation. These recipes are meant to guide and inspire you; ingredient lists are not written in stone. If you have a certain herb, vegetable, or other ingredient that is fresher or better suited to your needs, feel free to substitute.

Once you've decided on a recipe or menu, read through the recipes thoroughly before planning your shopping list. All great dishes start with the best ingredients— so take time at the market or local farm-stand to select the highest quality products you can find.

Whenever possible, buy from local growers and producers, which helps support and encourage sustainability within our communities and environment.

Before you begin cooking in your kitchen, read through the recipes once more to make sure you understand each step. Then, do what chefs at The Stephanie Inn do— prepare whatever you can ahead of time. For example, if a recipe calls for two cups of chopped tomatoes—chop them ahead and set them aside in a little bowl. If you need to cut beef or seafood into serving portions, do that ahead as well. Preparing all the necessary ingredients before you begin cooking adds to your enjoyment, satisfaction, and timeliness in cooking the meal.

THE STORY OF CANNON BEACH

Right outside the doors of The Stephanie Inn, the Pacific Ocean surges. Host to more than two hundred species of edible fish and shellfish, including halibut, salmon, tuna, mussels, clams, and crab, the Pacific Ocean is the pulse of Cannon Beach.

Eons ago, with a series of catastrophic events—earthquakes, volcanoes, tsunamis, the thrusting up of the coastal mountain range, landslides, and erosion—the geological formation of Cannon Beach began. The result is one of the most spectacular coastal landscapes in the world. Two famous seastacks, Haystack Rock and Silver Point Rock, were created during that tumultuous period, along with the two headlands that define the town's nine-mile stretch of beach—Silver Point (formerly known as Sylvan Point) to the south and Tillamook Head to the north.

Haystack Rock

Depending on the season and the prevailing winds, the Pacific Ocean can be as placid as an alpine lake or as violent as a hurricane. Summer days are marked by long spells of calm tides and sunshine, while fall and winter often approach with a vengeance, bringing mighty sou'westers that pound the shore with 80- to 100-mile-per-hour winds. During the storms, charcoal black clouds as voluptuous as full-blown roses race across the darkening sky, while eddies of salty mist spiral toward the inland mountains. The thundering roar of the ocean is broken only by the piercing cry of gulls overhead.

NATIVE BEGINNINGS AND ADVENTUROUS QUESTS

Less than two hundred years ago, Native Americans, including the Clatsop, Chinook and Tillamook tribes, lived along these shores, where they gathered native berries, fished for salmon and rockfish and collected clams and mussels. The gnarled spruce trees they camped beneath, the fire-pits where they cooked, and the fresh water springs from which they drank still exist. The Natives called the ocean, "the river with one bank."

The quest to reach the shores of this ocean by European explorers began in the early sixteenth century, when the Portuguese explorer Ferdinand Magellan led a Spanish expedition by sea to explore the world. It was on this journey that Magellan discovered and named the Pacific Ocean. He also brought back reports of a great river in the West, now known as the Columbia.

In 1543 the quest for the Columbia River began in earnest, with many explorers, including Juan Cabrillo and Bruno Heceta, searching in vain. In May of 1792, Captain Robert Gray, who was trading beads and buttons with the Northwest Native Americans for fur pelts to sell in China, was the first to cross the treacherous Columbia Bar and enter the great Columbia, thanks to fortuitously calm seas and the right tidal conditions.

Thomas Jefferson, during his tenure as the third president of the United States (1801 – 1809), became determined to find an overland route to reach the Columbia River. He sent his secretary, Captain Meriwether Lewis, and Lewis's friend, Captain William Clark, on a long journey to plot an overland route and to make notes of the plants, animals, and people they discovered. The Lewis and Clark Expedition started along the shores of the Missouri River and moved west to the shores of the Columbia River by the fall of 1805, enduring many hardships along the way. At the mouth of the great river, they set up a winter camp, Fort Clatsop, named for the local Indians.

In 1806, desperate for food and oil following a long, wet winter, Lewis and Clark heard of a beached whale south of Tillamook Head. Clark set out with a team of 12 men and their female guide, Sacagawea, in search of the whale. At the time, the south bank of Tillamook Head, one of the largest headlands jutting from the shore, was the site of many Indian villages. This area is now known as Indian Beach and Ecola Park. It was there, in l806, that the party led by Clark first saw Cannon Beach. Clark wrote in his journal: "From this point, I beheld the grandest and most pleasing prospect my eyes ever surveyed."

Clark and his troop proceeded down the Head and across the creek at the north end of Cannon Beach, which he called E Co-La ("whale" in the native dialect). There, Clark and his party found the skeleton of a 105-foot-long whale. Nearby, natives were boiling blubber and harvesting whale meat. After purchasing some 300 pounds of blubber and a few gallons of oil, the party headed back across the creek and followed the long, treacherous trail back to Fort Clatsop.

Cannon Beach Rediscovered

A century later the area now known as Cannon Beach was rediscovered. The development of the towns of Astoria and Seaside to the north and Arch Cape and Tillamook to the south brought people to the area who wondered about what lay between. By 1890, Astoria, with 11 salmon canneries, 47 saloons, and over 9,000 people was the third largest city in Oregon. Several popular hotels were built in Seaside, just north of Cannon Beach, and to the south, there was a thriving dairy industry in Tillamook. The logging industry had also picked up pace. With so many new settlers, increased interest in visiting the spectacular coastline that lay in between the north and south coasts was only natural—but there were no roads, yet.

In the years to follow, railroads were developed between Astoria, Young's Bay, and Seaside. More hotels were built, mainly in Seaside, and a rough road following an old Indian trail between Seaside and Cannon Beach was finally opened. Called the Elk Creek Toll Road, the road was notorious for its 111 curves and muddy paths. A sign at the beginning of the road read: "Single Horse, Mule or Ass/25 cents, Four Horse Team/$1, Cattle Driven/25 cents, Sheep and Hogs/10 cents."

Locals gather at the cannon.

The first homesteader in Cannon Beach (then called Elk Creek) built his home near the creek around 1850. By the 1870s there were several more homesteaders living in rustic cabins built of local timber. When the toll road finally opened, and people had access to Cannon Beach, they were eager to visit and establish homestead claims in one of the most beautiful coastal areas they had ever seen.

Several dozen families and a few bachelors from the British Isles (known as "remittance men") filed homestead claims between Tolovana Park and Cape Falcon. They had plenty of timber for fuel and for building cabins. Food was plentiful—elk, deer, bear, duck, berries, fish, and shellfish were widely available. Small gardens, plus a few cows and chickens provided the remaining necessities.

By the early 1900s, groups of neighbors from Portland had begun building small beach cottages in Cannon Beach. To be near their friends, they often built their cabins very close to their neighbors. One of the first of these neighborhoods was known as the "Brooklyn Camp," named for the cottage owners from the Brooklyn neighborhood of Portland. Another early settlement was located in Tolovana Park, at the Wave Crest plot, near Brallier Road. Additional developments included the Silver Point Cliffs (formerly known as Sylvan Point), Haystack Rock Park, Arch Cape Park, Antler Lodge, and the Elk Creek parcels. Platted in 1903, the hundred-foot oceanfront Elk Creek parcels sold for $100 apiece. Someone even tried to file a claim on Haystack Rock, intending to build homes on it, but fortunately the claim was denied.

A Land of Strong Individuals

During these early years, some remarkably strong and heroic people emerged in the region—people who embodied the courageous character of many of the early settlers and the spirit that still shines in many of the locals who now live in Cannon Beach. They were people of dignity, strength, enormous patience, and courage. Two of these people, Mary and John Gerritse, settled in Arch Cape (then known as Cannon Beach). John, who was born in Holland, became the mail carrier between

Seaside and Tillamook, a round-trip route that took at least one week to complete. In 1897, after marrying John, Mary took over her husband's job of carrying the mail. For 15 years, riding her horse, Prince, she delivered the mail between Seaside and Tillamook, enduring all the hardships the coast had to offer.

During the winters, high tides, gale winds, and muddy trails were extremely dangerous. One time, rounding the head of Neahkahnie Mountain, Mary's horse slipped and fell, sliding over 150 feet to the bottom of a steep canyon. More than 300 feet below her, at the bottom of another steep canyon, the ocean waves crashed against the rock. After quieting her horse, Mary spent two hours breaking the bushes down so that Prince, who had broken a rib, could stand up safely. Mary hiked through the woods and forest into Cannon Beach to deliver the mail with Prince following her to town and back.

In 1879, another group of courageous people emerged when construction began on the Tillamook Lighthouse (later known as Terrible Tilly), just north of Cannon Beach. One of the most treacherous bodies of water in the world, the Columbia Bar had been nicknamed the "graveyard of the Pacific." In order to help ships find their way around Tillamook Head, a lighthouse was erected on Tillamook

Tillamook Lighthouse

Rock, due west of what is now Ecola Park. After many failed attempts at fighting gale winds and surging waves, the workers finally managed to land on the rock to build the lighthouse. While the men worked on the lighthouse, the rock was often enveloped by huge waves that hurled rocks and boulders over the construction site. The brave workers clung to the rock for their lives and persevered. The lighthouse was eventually finished, offering a beacon of hope and light to ships from around the world.

WHY "CANNON BEACH?"

Thirty-four years prior to the construction of the Tillamook Lighthouse, the cannon from which Cannon Beach eventually got its name washed ashore. In 1845, a U.S. Navy schooner, the Shark, went down trying to cross the bar at the mouth of the Columbia River near Astoria. The damaged ship, armed with three cannons, drifted south and eventually washed ashore below Hug Point at what is now the town of Arch Cape. One of the cannons was eventually rescued and placed in a nearby creek bed for safekeeping.

As the blackberries and weeds grew around it, the cannon disappeared from view, and it was not spotted again until 1884. Former mail carrier John Gerritse then harnessed his team of horses and they hauled the cannon to a place in front of Gerritse's Austin House. In 1965, the cannon was purchased by Mel Goodwin and moved to a site on Highway 101, which had been donated by a local logger, George Van Vleet. Later, in 1989, the cannon was moved to the Heritage Museum in Astoria, Oregon, near where the shipwreck had occurred. In 1969, with the opening of the Cannon Beach Historical Society, the original cannon was moved once more to the town bearing its name. Three replicas of the cannon were made and two of them were placed at the north and south entrances of Cannon Beach, respectively. The remaining replica resides at the original site on Highway 101 in Arch Cape.

The name Cannon Beach was originally applied to what is now called Arch Cape, which is where the cannon washed ashore. In 1910, when the first post office was established in what is now Cannon Beach, the town was called Ecola, as first named by Lewis and Clark. Several years later, the original Cannon Beach changed its name to Arch Cape. Because of confusion regarding postal service between the town of Ecola at the coast and the town of Eola in the Willamette Valley, the Ecola locals voted to rename their town Cannon Beach.

Confusing? Yes. But Cannon Beach it became, and it has become a favorite year 'round seaside destination for people from around the world.

At right, Jay Schwehr has been the Cannon Beach lamplighter for over 30 years; below, a Cannon Beach street scene circa 1950.

A Glossary of Terms

We suggest that you familiarize yourself with descriptions and definitions before you use the recipes in this book.

Butter:
Unsalted, unless otherwise specified (if using salted butter, adjust seasonings accordingly)

Cooking oil:
Canola oil, peanut oil, or olive oil. Canola oil is the preferred oil for many dishes, as it imparts a neutral taste and reaches a high cooking temperature before smoking, as does peanut oil. Olive oil is mostly used for salad dressings and marinades.

Deglaze:
Adding an acidic liquid, such as wine or vinegar, to a hot pan in which an item has been cooked, then stirring in the liquid to dissolve and incorporate the flavorful solids sticking to the bottom of the pan.

Freshly Ground Pepper:
Black or white peppercorns.

Julienne:
To cut into thin strips like matchsticks

Salt:
Kosher salt or sea salt

Season with Salt and Pepper:
Sprinkle liberally with kosher salt and freshly ground pepper (black or white peppercorns).

Sugar:
Granulated sugar, unless otherwise specified.

Zest:
The grated rind of a citrus fruit.

STEPHANIE INN GRANOLA

4 cups rolled oats

3/4 cup blanched, slivered almonds

3/4 cup unsweetened, shredded coconut

1/4 cup sesame seeds

1/4 cup sunflower seeds

3/4 cup honey

1/2 cup canola oil or safflower oil

1 cup hot tap water

1 cup dried cranberries

1 cup raisins

THIS CRUNCHY, FRUITY GRANOLA IS A FAVORITE ELEMENT OF THE DAILY BREAKFAST BUFFET AT THE INN. THE SWEET-TART DRIED CRANBERRIES COME FROM OREGON COAST CRANBERRY BOGS. DURING HARVEST THE WATERS OF THE BOGS ARE RED WITH BOBBING BERRIES. THE GRANOLA MAY BE STORED IN AN AIRTIGHT CONTAINER FOR UP TO 2 WEEKS.

Preheat the oven to 350° F.

In a large mixing bowl, combine the oats, almonds, coconut, sesame seeds and sunflower seeds. In a separate bowl, stir together the honey, oil, and hot water. Pour the liquid mixture into the oat mixture. Spread the mixture over two ungreased baking pans and bake for about 15 to 20 minutes, stirring often. Bake until the mixture is dry and light golden in color. Let cool to room temperature and then stir in the dried cranberries and raisins. Serve with milk.

SERVES 12 (APPROXIMATELY)

STRAWBERRY FRENCH TOAST

2 cups fresh strawberries, cleaned, hulled and sliced

1/2 cup powdered sugar

Optional: 2 tablespoons Grand Marnier or other orange-flavored liqueur

5 eggs

1/2 cup half-and-half

1/2 cup milk

1/2 teaspoon ground cinnamon

1/4 teaspoon ground cloves

Zest of 1 lemon

3/4 cup brown sugar

Canola or safflower oil, as needed, to oil griddle

8-16 slices bread (1/2-inch thick)

Real maple syrup to taste

FRESH OREGON STRAWBERRIES ARE THE ULTIMATE—JUICY, DEEP RED TO THE CORE, AND EXCEPTIONALLY FLAVORFUL. WHEN STRAWBERRIES ARE IN SEASON, THIS IS THE BEST, TOPPED OFF WITH REAL MAPLE SYRUP. IF STRAWBERRIES ARE NOT IN SEASON, SUBSTITUTE OTHER FRESH FRUIT, SUCH AS PEACHES OR RASPBERRIES. THE STEPHANIE INN CHEFS USE DAY-OLD HOUSE-BREAD. SEE THE RECIPE INDEX FOR STEPHANIE HOUSE BREAD, OR USE ANY FLAVORFUL, CRUSTY WHITE BREAD.

In a mixing bowl, toss the strawberries, the powdered sugar and the optional Grand Marnier; set aside.

In a separate bowl, beat the eggs with a wire whisk until well-mixed. Whisk in the half-and-half, milk, cinnamon, cloves, lemon zest, and brown sugar, mixing well.

Preheat a griddle or large non-stick pan to medium heat. When hot, brush the griddle with oil. Immerse the bread slices in the egg mixture until the bread has absorbed the liquid on both sides (about 15 seconds). Drain excess liquid from the bread by dragging each slice against the sides of the bowl. Bake the toast on the hot griddle for about 2 minutes per side, or until golden.

To serve: Top each piece of toast with fresh strawberries and maple syrup.

SERVES 4

The Stephanie House Bread

THE STEPHANIE'S HOUSE BREAD

2   tablespoons dry yeast

1/4 cup sugar

2   teaspoons salt

2   cups milk, lukewarm

8   cups all-purpose unbleached
     flour, approximately (or use
     part whole wheat flour in place
     of white flour)

1   egg, beaten, room temperature

2   tablespoons butter, melted

1   egg, beaten

Kosher salt

IF YOU HAPPEN BY THE STEPHANIE INN KITCHEN IN THE EARLY AFTERNOON, THE INTOXICATING AROMA OF WARM BREAD FRESH FROM THE OVEN WILL UNDOUBTEDLY SEDUCE YOU. SERVED TOASTED AT BREAKFAST, TOPPED WITH BUTTER, MARMALADE OR STRAWBERRY JAM, THIS BREAD IS SUBLIME. AT DINNER, IT IS THE PERFECT ACCOMPANIMENT TO A BOWL OF CREAMY SOUP OR SEAFOOD CHOWDER. THE CHEFS AT THE STEPHANIE ARE VERY CREATIVE WITH THIS RECIPE, ADDING FLAVORINGS, SUCH AS, ROASTED GARLIC, SUN-DRIED TOMATOES, KALAMATA OLIVES, HERBS OR GRATED CHEESE. OFTEN, THEY SPRINKLE THE BREAD WITH POPPY SEEDS, SESAME SEEDS, OR KOSHER SALT. USE YOUR IMAGINATION AND FAVORITE FLAVORINGS TO COME UP WITH YOUR OWN VERSION.

In a large mixing bowl, mix together the yeast, sugar and salt. Slowly add the warm milk, without stirring. Allow the mixture to stand for about 5 minutes, until the yeast begins to bubble. Stir the yeast mixture with a wooden spoon until creamy; then stir in 2 cups of the flour. Cover the bowl with plastic wrap and let the mixture rise in a warm place for about 1 hour, or until it has doubled in bulk. Stir the mixture down and allow it to rise again for about 45 minutes.

Mix in the beaten egg and melted butter; then gradually add the remaining flour and mix until the dough comes away from the sides of the bowl. Add more flour if necessary. Turn the dough onto a floured surface and knead for about 10 minutes, until the dough is soft and satiny, adding flour as necessary.

MAKES 2 LOAVES

Place the dough in a clean, oiled mixing bowl and cover with plastic wrap. Allow it to rise for about 1 hour, or until doubled in bulk. Turn the dough onto a floured surface and divide in two. Flour your hands and shape the dough into two round loaves by folding each piece of dough in toward its center. Shape into free-form oblong loaves, and place, seam side down, on a well-greased baking pan or a baking pan covered with parchment paper. Cover each loaf lightly with plastic wrap and set aside in a warm place to rise for about 30 minutes.

Meanwhile, preheat the oven to 375° F. To judge when the dough is ready to bake, press it lightly with your finger. The imprint should spring back almost immediately.

Brush the loaves lightly with egg wash and sprinkle with kosher salt.

Place the loaves in the preheated oven and bake for about 35 minutes, or until a fragrant aroma emerges and the golden loaves sound hollow when tapped with your finger (a thermometer inserted in the middle of a loaf should register 190° F.) Let the bread cool on a baking rack for at least 15 minutes before cutting and serving.

BLACKBERRY SOUR CREAM COFFEE CAKE

1/3 cup butter, softened

3/4 cup sugar

2 eggs, room temperature

3/4 cup sour cream

1 teaspoon vanilla extract

3/4 cup all-purpose flour

1 teaspoon baking powder

1 teaspoon cinnamon

1/2 teaspoon salt

3/4 cup chopped pecans or walnuts

1 cup fresh or frozen blackberries

THE LUSH OREGON COAST ENVIRONMENT PROVIDES THE PERFECT HABITAT FOR BLACKBERRIES OF ALL KINDS—FROM TINY, NATIVE, WILD BLACKBERRIES TO THE NOW ESTABLISHED HIMALAYAN AND EVERGREEN BLACKBERRIES. WHILE ALL HAVE THEIR FOLLOWERS, IT IS THE TINY, SEEDLESS NATIVE BERRIES (OFTEN GROWING IN ELUSIVE LOCATIONS) THAT ARE MOST COVETED. NO BIGGER THAN THE TIP OF A LITTLE FINGER, ONE WILD BERRY CAN PACK MORE FLAVOR THAN A CUP OF THE OTHER VARIETIES.

IF FRESH BLACKBERRIES ARE NOT IN SEASON, YOU CAN SUBSTITUTE OTHER FRESH BERRIES, SUCH AS BLUEBERRIES OR HUCKLEBERRIES, OR USE DRIED FRUITS SUCH AS RAISINS, CURRANTS, OR DRIED CHERRIES.

Preheat the oven to 350° F.

Oil a bundt pan or cake pan and sprinkle lightly with sugar.

In a mixing bowl, whip the butter at medium speed until creamy. Reduce the speed to low and gradually add the sugar, mixing well. Add the eggs, one at a time, mixing well, then add the sour cream and vanilla. Increase the speed to medium and mix well, scraping down the sides of the bowl as needed.

Place the flour, baking powder, cinnamon, and salt in a mixing bowl and, using a wire whisk or spoon, mix thoroughly. Add the flour mixture to the butter mixture in several increments, mixing well after each addition. Gently stir in the pecans and berries. Pour the batter into the prepared pan and bake for about 30 or 40 minutes, or until a toothpick inserted in the center comes out clean.

FILLS ONE BUNDT PAN OR
ONE 10-INCH SPRING-FORM PAN

BUTTERMILK MUFFINS
APPLES & CINNAMON

YOU WON'T BE ABLE TO RESIST THESE TENDER MUFFINS. NOTHING QUITE BEATS THE GOOD OLD-FASHIONED TASTE OF APPLES AND CINNAMON. HERE, THEY ARE COMBINED IN A TANGY BUTTERMILK MUFFIN BATTER. GET READY FOR A WONDERFUL AROMA WHEN YOU PULL THESE WARM, MOIST MUFFINS FRESH FROM THE OVEN. AT THE STEPHANIE INN, THE CHEFS OFTEN SUBSTITUTE OTHER INGREDIENTS, SUCH AS BANANAS AND WALNUTS OR FRESH BERRIES OR CHERRIES AND ALMONDS. TRY YOUR FAVORITE COMBINATIONS TO CREATE YOUR OWN VERSION OF THESE POPULAR MUFFINS.

Preheat oven to 350° F.

Grease a 12-cup muffin tin, or line paper muffin cups.

In a large mixing bowl, whisk the beaten eggs with the sugar until the sugar has dissolved. Whisk in the oil and buttermilk, mixing well. In a separate bowl, whisk together the flour, baking powder, salt, and cinnamon. Quickly mix the dry ingredients into the egg mixture. Stir in the diced apple. Distribute the batter into the prepared muffin tin and sprinkle the top of each muffin with cinnamon and sugar. Bake for about 15 to 20 minutes, or until the muffins are golden on top and a knife inserted in the center comes out clean.

2	eggs, beaten
1¾	cups sugar
1	cup canola or safflower oil
1	cup buttermilk
2	cups all-purpose flour
1	teaspoon baking powder
1/2	teaspoon salt
1/2	teaspoon cinnamon
1	apple, peeled and diced
1	teaspoon cinnamon
2	tablespoons sugar

MAKES 12 (2-INCH) MUFFINS

STEPHANIE INN SCONES

2½ cups all-purpose flour
1/2 cup sugar
1 tablespoon baking powder
1/2 teaspoon salt

1 cup chopped fresh or dried
fruit, nuts, chocolate chips
or a combination of flavors

1¼ cups heavy cream
(approximately)

MOIST, RICH, AND TENDER, THESE FLAVORFUL SCONES ARE A FAVORITE BREAKFAST TREAT AT THE STEPHANIE INN. DEPENDING ON THE SEASON, THEY MIGHT BE FLAVORED WITH CHOPPED NUTS, DRIED FRUITS SUCH AS CURRANTS, DRIED APRICOTS, DRIED CHERRIES, RAISINS, FRESH MANGO, OR BLACKBERRIES. THE SECRET TO MAKING TENDER SCONES IS TO WORK THE DOUGH AS LITTLE AS POSSIBLE AFTER ADDING THE CREAM—JUST UNTIL IT BINDS TOGETHER AND CAN BE ROLLED OUT ON A LIGHTLY FLOURED SURFACE.

Preheat the oven to 350° F.

In a large mixing bowl, whisk or stir the dry ingredients together, mixing thoroughly. Stir in the fruit or nuts, and then slowly stir in the cream, just until the mixture binds together. Turn the dough onto a lightly floured surface and gently pat the mixture into a round or square shape. Sprinkle with flour and roll to approximately 1/2" thickness. Cut into rounds, triangles, or squares. Place on a greased baking sheet and brush with additional heavy cream. Sprinkle with sugar and bake for about 15 to 20 minutes, or until lightly golden.

MAKES 12 SCONES

BUTTERMILK-CHEDDAR CHEESE BISCUITS
SAUSAGE & BACON GRAVY

BUTTERMILK-CHEDDAR CHEESE BISCUITS

2   cups all-purpose flour

2   teaspoons baking powder

1   teaspoon salt

1/3 cup butter, chilled and cut into
     1/4-inch pieces

1   cup grated, sharp cheddar
     cheese

3/4 cup buttermilk (approximately)

DURING A WINTER STORM AT THE COAST, WHEN THE RAIN IS SLEETING SIDEWAYS AND HURRICANE FORCE WINDS ARE POUNDING THE SHORE, NOTHING IS MORE COMFORTING THAN A HEARTY BREAKFAST OF GOOD OL' BISCUITS AND GRAVY. AT THE STEPHANIE INN, YOU'LL FIND THIS RATHER ELEGANT RENDITION OF THE CLASSIC DISH. LEFTOVERS WILL KEEP UP TO 2 DAYS, REFRIGERATED. SIMPLY REHEAT TO SERVE.

Preheat the oven to 350° F.

To make the Buttermilk-Cheddar Cheese Biscuits: In a mixing bowl or food processor, combine the flour, baking powder and salt, mixing thoroughly. Cut in the chilled butter until it is reduced to pea-sized bits. Add the cheddar cheese followed by the buttermilk and mix until the dough just binds together; add more buttermilk as needed. Remember, the secret to making flaky biscuits is a light hand; don't over-mix the dough.

Transfer the dough to a floured surface and roll out to 1-inch thickness. Cut into small (1½-inch to 2-inch rounds or squares) and place on a lightly greased baking sheet. Bake about 10 to 12 minutes, or until lightly golden. Transfer to cooling racks.

SERVES 6

To make the Sausage & Bacon Gravy: Make a "roux" by melting the 2 tablespoons butter in a small saucepan over medium-high heat. Gradually whisk in the 2 tablespoons of flour, stirring constantly. Lower the heat to medium and cook about 1 minute, until the roux you've created has a nutty aroma and golden color. Set the mixture aside and let it cool to room temperature.

In a heavy saucepan over medium heat, combine the chopped onion, heavy cream, and cream cheese. Whisk often, until the cream cheese is melted and all the ingredients are combined.

Using a wire whisk, mix the roux into the cream mixture, a bit at a time, until the gravy reaches the desired thickness. Stir in the cooked sausage and bacon, mixing well. Season to taste with salt and pepper.

To serve: Slice the biscuits in half horizontally and top with the hot gravy.

SAUSAGE & BACON GRAVY

2	tablespoons butter
2	tablespoons all-purpose flour
1/2	cup chopped onion
2	cups heavy cream
1/4	cup cream cheese, softened
1	teaspoon Tabasco sauce
1	pound ground pork or chicken and apple sausage, cooked and drained
3	strips cooked bacon, crumbled

Salt and freshly ground black pepper to taste

2   tablespoons butter

1   teaspoon dried oregano

1   teaspoon cumin

1/4 cup diced onion

1/4 cup diced red bell pepper

1   cup chopped spinach (remove stems before chopping)

1   cup chorizo or other breakfast sausage, cooked and drained

LIGHTLY SCRAMBLED EGGS

2   teaspoons butter

1   teaspoon vegetable oil

4   eggs

Salt and freshly ground black pepper to taste

4   eight-inch flour tortillas

1/2 cup grated sharp cheddar cheese

GARNISH

1/2 cup diced tomato

1/4 cup sour cream

1/2 cup Mango Salsa (see Recipe Index)

1   ripe avocado, peeled and sliced

SERVES 4

BREAKFAST WRAPS

SOFT FLOUR TORTILLAS ARE FILLED WITH A TASTY MIXTURE OF SCRAMBLED EGGS, CHORIZO, SPINACH, PEPPERS, CHEESE AND SPICES, THEN BAKED UNTIL THE CHEESE IS MELTED. SPICE THEM UP EVEN MORE WITH A LITTLE HOT SALSA.

Preheat the oven to 350° F.

Melt the butter in a medium skillet over medium-high heat. Stir in the oregano, cumin, onion, and bell pepper. Sauté about 7 minutes, or until the vegetables have softened. Stir in the spinach and cook just until it has wilted, about 3 minutes. Drain any liquid from the mixture and set it aside to cool slightly.

To scramble the eggs: Heat the butter and the oil until bubbling in a medium, non-stick skillet over medium-high heat. Meanwhile, whisk the eggs together with a fork or wire whisk. Pour the eggs into the prepared skillet and immediately reduce the heat to low. Stir the eggs lightly and constantly with a rubber spatula, just until they firm up. Remove the eggs from the heat and transfer them to a clean bowl.

Warm the tortillas on a griddle, or in a preheated oven just until pliable, about 2 to 3 minutes. Lay the tortillas out on a clean surface and top each tortilla with 1/4 of the vegetable mixture, 1/4 of the scrambled eggs, 1/4 of the chorizo, and 1 tablespoon of the grated cheese. Roll up the tortillas and place with the seam side down on a lightly oiled baking sheet.

Place the wraps in the oven and bake about 15 minutes, or until heated through. Sprinkle with the remaining cheddar cheese and replace in the oven to bake until the cheese is melted.

To serve: Arrange wraps on pre-warmed plates and top with diced tomato, sour cream, Mango Salsa, and sliced avocado.

CHEF'S TIP

These breakfast wraps can be prepared up to 2 hours in advance. Cover with plastic wrap to keep the tortillas moist and store in the refrigerator until needed.

STEPHANIE INN SCOTCH EGGS

THIS UNIQUE RECIPE IS A FAVORITE AMONG THE STEPHANIE INN GUESTS. MOST OF THE INGREDIENTS CAN BE PREPARED AHEAD OF TIME, MAKING THIS AN EASY YET ELEGANT SHOW-STOPPER FOR YOUR NEXT BREAKFAST OR BRUNCH. SERVE THE EGGS WITH HASH BROWNS, FRESH SCONES OR TOAST, AND HOT COFFEE OR TEA. ON SPECIAL OCCASIONS, YOU MIGHT SERVE MIMOSAS (ORANGE JUICE MIXED WITH CHAMPAGNE AND A DASH OF GRAND MARNIER).

Preheat the oven to 350° F.

Oil a baking sheet.

Peel the hard-boiled eggs and set them on paper towels to dry. Divide the sausage into 4 equal pieces and shape each piece into 4 thin patties (about 1/4-inch thick) to wrap around each egg. Set each egg in the center of a sausage patty and fold the sides up and over the egg, pressing firmly to seal the packet.

Place the egg packets on the oiled baking sheet. Drizzle the packets with maple syrup and sprinkle them with garlic powder, salt, and pepper. Bake for about 20 minutes, or until the sausage is fully cooked.

To serve: Slice each packet in half lengthwise and place on warmed serving plates. Garnish with grated cheese. Add a dash of paprika to each half.

4	eggs, hard-boiled
1	pound ground pork sausage
1/4	cup real maple syrup
1/2	teaspoon garlic powder
1	teaspoon kosher salt

Freshly ground black pepper to taste

3/4	cup grated sharp cheddar cheese

Paprika for garnish

CHEF'S TIP

For perfectly cooked hard-boiled eggs, place the eggs in a saucepan and cover with luke-warm water. Place the pan over medium-high heat and bring to a boil. Once the water boils, keep the eggs simmering for 12 minutes. Immediately submerge the eggs in ice water until they are cool enough to handle.

SERVES 4

BREAKFAST QUICHE

Treat your friends and family at home to a Stephanie Inn breakfast. Served with freshly baked scones or muffins, hash browns, and just-squeezed orange juice, this crustless quiche is a delicious breakfast or brunch entrée.

2 tablespoons vegetable oil

1 garlic clove, minced

1 small onion, diced

1 cup spinach rinsed, dried, stems removed and sliced into 1-inch pieces

1 cup diced vegetables (mushrooms, asparagus, bell peppers, beans)

Salt and freshly ground pepper to taste

6 to 8 ounces Italian sausage or pepper bacon, cooked and broken into bite-size pieces

6 eggs, beaten

1/2 cup grated sharp cheddar cheese

Optional garnish: salsa and sour cream

Preheat the oven to 350° F.

Grease a 9- or 10-inch pie pan (preferably non-stick).

Heat the oil in a large skillet over medium heat. Add the garlic, onion, spinach and diced vegetables, and cook, stirring often, until the onions are tender, about 15 minutes. Remove the vegetables from the heat, season with salt and pepper to taste, and set aside.

Meanwhile, whisk the eggs thoroughly in a separate bowl. Distribute the vegetable mixture evenly over the bottom of the greased pan. Pour the beaten eggs over the vegetables. Place the pan in the oven and bake for about 15 to 20 minutes, or just until the eggs are set.

Turn on the broiler. Top the egg mixture with the grated cheese and place 6 inches below the broiler element to melt the cheese; watch closely.

To serve: Garnish with salsa and sour cream as desired and serve hot.

SERVES 8

OVEN-ROASTED POTATOES

AT THE STEPHANIE INN, THIS IS A FAVORITE ACCOMPANIMENT FOR FRESHLY SCRAMBLED EGGS SERVED WITH FRESH FRUIT, SCONES OR MUFFINS. SIMPLY MIX THE INGREDIENTS TOGETHER AND BAKE IN THE OVEN UNTIL GOLDEN. TURN THE OVEN TO LOW AND KEEP THE POTATOES WARM UNTIL READY TO SERVE.

Preheat the oven to 350° F.

Oil a baking sheet.

Toss all the ingredients together in a mixing bowl. Spread the potatoes on the oiled baking sheet. Bake for about 25 minutes, stirring occasionally, or until the potatoes are tender and golden.

4	medium red-skinned or Yukon Gold potatoes, diced
1	tablespoon salt
2	tablespoons vegetable oil
1	garlic clove, minced
1	small red onion, diced
1	teaspoon paprika
2	tablespoons fresh thyme, rosemary, or other aromatic herbs
3	tablespoons chopped fresh parsley for garnish

SERVES 6

POTATO PANCAKES

4 large russet potatoes,
   peeled and grated

3 large eggs

2 garlic cloves, minced

1/4 cup onion, grated

Salt and freshly ground black pepper
   to taste

Vegetable oil or butter as needed
   for frying

RAW, SHREDDED POTATOES ARE MIXED WITH BEATEN EGGS, SEASONED, AND FRIED UNTIL GOLDEN, LETTING THE EARTHY FLAVOR AND HEARTY TEXTURE OF THE POTATOES SHINE THROUGH. THE PANCAKES ARE DELICIOUS TOPPED WITH SOUR CREAM AND SPRINKLED WITH FRESH CHOPPED CHIVES OR SCALLIONS. AND DON'T FORGET GREAT ACCOMPANIMENTS—SCRAMBLED EGGS WITH CHEESE, FRESH FRUIT, AND SCONES OR HOT-BUTTERED TOAST.

Place the grated potatoes in a large colander and rinse in cold running water. Squeeze the moisture from the potatoes by pressing down firmly with your hands. In a large mixing bowl, add the eggs and whisk until creamy. Add the garlic, grated onion, and grated potatoes. Season the mixture with salt and pepper.

Heat the oil in a large, heavy-bottomed skillet over medium heat. When sizzling, drop 1/4-cup increments of the potato-cake batter into the skillet and fry until golden on both sides, about 7 to 10 minutes per side. Transfer the potato cakes to a platter and keep them warm in a low oven until ready to serve.

SERVES 8

BEEF TENDERLOIN CROSTINI
ROASTED GARLIC, ROASTED BEETS & DRIED CHERRIES

4   small beets

12 garlic cloves, peeled

2   tablespoons olive oil

1   baguette, sliced 1/2-inch thick
    (20 slices)

Olive oil or melted butter

1   tablespoon olive oil

8   ounces beef tenderloin,
    trimmed of fat

Salt and freshly ground black pepper
    to taste

1/2 cup dried cherries

SLATHERED IN ROASTED GARLIC, THESE CRISP BITE-SIZE PIECES OF TOASTED BREAD ARE TOPPED WITH SWEET ROASTED BEETS, TENDER SLICES OF FILET MIGNON, AND DRIED CHERRIES. WHEN SERVING, CONSIDER POURING A RICH, FRUITY PINOT NOIR, SYRAH OR MERLOT TO HIGHLIGHT THE FLAVORS IN THIS DISH.

REMEMBER TO ALLOW TIME TO ROAST THE BEETS AND GARLIC — ABOUT ONE HOUR. THE ROASTING MAY BE DONE UP TO ONE DAY IN ADVANCE.

Preheat the oven to 350° F.

Toss the beets and garlic cloves in olive oil and place in the oven in two separate ovenproof pans. Roast the garlic for about 20-30 minutes, until tender. Remove it from the oven. Continue roasting the beets until they are tender when pierced with a fork, approximately 45 minutes total. Set aside until the beets are cool enough to handle, then cut them into 1/4-inch thick slices.

Brush both sides of the bread slices with olive oil or butter and season one side of each slice with salt and pepper. Place them on a baking pan and bake for about 10 minutes, or until crisp and golden. Set aside.

Heat 2 tablespoons of olive oil in a small skillet over medium-high heat. Season the beef tenderloin with salt and pepper and add to the hot oil. Sear the beef, turning occasionally and cooking until rare (115 – 120° F). Let the beef rest for 2 to 3 minutes, then slice into bite-size, 1/4-inch thick pieces.

To assemble and serve: Smear the roasted garlic onto the toasted bread slices with a knife or spatula. Top with a slice of roasted beet, followed by slices of beef tenderloin. Garnish each crostini with several dried cherries.

SERVES 10 TO 12

Tuna & Salmon Tostadas

LEMON-AVOCADO PURÉE
Makes about 1 cup

1   ripe avocado, peeled

Juice of 1/2 lemon

1/4 cup water

Salt and freshly ground black pepper
     to taste

MANGO SALSA
Makes about 2 cups

4   tomatillos, peeled and diced

2   garlic cloves, minced

1   jalapeno pepper, seeded
    and diced

1/4 cup water

3   Roma tomatoes, diced

1   mango, peeled and diced

1/2 red onion, diced

2   tablespoons chopped
    fresh cilantro

Juice of 1 lime

Salt and freshly ground black pepper
     to taste

TUNA & SALMON TOSTADAS
LEMON-AVOCADO PURÉE & MANGO SALSA

FOR THIS TASTY APPETIZER, THE CHEFS AT THE STEPHANIE INN USE A COOKIE CUTTER TO CUT TORTILLAS INTO 3-INCH ROUNDS. AFTER FRYING, THE TORTILLA ROUNDS ARE SET ON A POOL OF BLACK BEANS AND STACKED IN A DRAMATIC PRESENTATION WITH MANGO SALSA, GRILLED SALMON, AND TUNA. TOPPINGS OF FINELY SHREDDED, FRIED TORTILLAS (TORTILLA CONFETTI) AND MANGO SALSA ADD THE FINISHING TOUCH. FOLLOW THE CHEF'S EXAMPLE AS SHOWN IN THE PHOTOGRAPH.

Plan to prepare the Lemon Avocado Purée and Mango Salsa ahead. They will both keep up to 24 hours in the refrigerator.

To make the Lemon Avocado Purée: Place the avocado, lemon juice, and water in a food processor or blender. Blend until the mixture forms a thick purée. Transfer to a clean bowl and season to taste with salt and pepper.

To make the Mango Salsa: Purée the tomatillos, garlic, and jalapeno pepper in the bowl of a food processor or blender. Combine the diced tomatoes, mango, onion, cilantro and lime juice in a mixing bowl. Stir in the tomatillo purée and season to taste with salt and pepper.

To prepare the Tuna and Salmon Tostadas: Preheat the oven to 300° F. Heat the vegetable oil in a skillet over medium heat. Using a 3" cookie cutter, cut the tortillas into 8 rounds. When the oil is hot, fry the tortillas one at a time, turning once, until crisp and golden on both sides. Drain the tortillas on paper towels and place in the oven to keep warm.

Heat the black beans in a saucepan. Season them with cumin and salt and pepper to taste. Keep warm. Meanwhile, preheat an electric or charcoal grill to medium-high heat. Season the salmon fillets with salt and pepper. Place on the hot grill and cook, turning several times, until the fish is just cooked through, about 6 to 8 minutes. Remove from the heat and set aside. Cook tuna to medium rate or desired doneness, approsimately 3 to 5 minutes.

To assemble and serve: Ladle the black beans onto a serving plate. Top the beans with a tortilla, then spread with a layer of shredded cabbage and cover with Mango Salsa. Lay the salmon over the top. Top the salmon with the second tortilla, followed by the tuna, more Mango Salsa, and a topping of shredded fried tortillas (optional). Drizzle with Lemon-Avocado Purée and pass extra salsa on the side.

TUNA & SALMON TOSTADAS

2	tablespoons vegetable oil
2	eight-inch corn tortillas
8	ounces salmon fillet, skinned, boned and sliced into 2-inch strips
8	ounces ahi tuna fillet, skinned, boned and sliced into 2-inch strips
1/2	cup shredded green cabbage
2	cups cooked black beans
1	teaspoon cumin

Salt and freshly ground black pepper to taste

Optional garnish:
    shredded, fried tortillas

SERVES 4 AS AN APPETIZER OR 2 AS A MAIN COURSE

TARTAR SAUCE

1   cup mayonnaise (preferably homemade)

2   tablespoons sweet pickle relish

2   teaspoons capers

1   teaspoon Worchestershire sauce

Tabasco sauce to taste

Salt and freshly ground black pepper to taste

4   ounces raw razor or geoduck clams, cleaned and chopped into 1/4-inch pieces (reserve 2 tablespoons clam juice)

BATTER:

1½   teaspoons baking powder

1/2   cup all-purpose flour

1/2   teaspoon salt

1/4   teaspoon freshly ground black pepper

Reserved 2 tablespoons clam juice

1/4   cup milk

2   cups canola or peanut oil, approximate

Lemon wedges

SERVES 4

NORTH COAST CLAM FRITTERS
TARTAR SAUCE

NORTHWEST RAZOR CLAMS OR GEODUCKS ARE THE CHEF'S FAVORITE CLAMS FOR THIS RECIPE, BUT ANY SWEET, FLAVORFUL CLAM CAN BE SUBSTITUTED. PLAN TO MAKE THE TARTAR SAUCE IN ADVANCE. IT CAN BE STORED, COVERED, IN THE REFRIGERATOR UP TO 3 DAYS.

To make the Tartar Sauce: Whisk all of the ingredients together in a bowl and season to taste with Tabasco sauce, salt and pepper.

To make the Fritters: In a mixing bowl, whisk together the baking powder, flour, salt, and pepper. In a separate mixing bowl, stir together the chopped clams, clam juice, and milk. Stir the flour mixture into the clams, mixing thoroughly.

Preheat the oil to 375° F in a large, heavy-bottomed skillet or deep-fat fryer. Working in small batches, drop the fritter batter into the hot oil (2 tablespoons at a time). Turn often, cooking until the fritters are golden and cooked through. Drain on paper towels and serve hot with tartar sauce and lemon wedges.

ROASTED EGGPLANT CAVIAR
HONEY & CHILI PASTE

SERVE THIS FLAVORFUL EGGPLANT CAVIAR ON CRACKERS OR CROSTINI AS AN APPETIZER, OR TOSS WITH FRESHLY COOKED PASTA FOR A DELICIOUS VEGETARIAN ENTRÉE. THIS CAN BE PREPARED UP TO 2 DAYS AHEAD OF SERVING.

Preheat the oven to 350° F.

Roast the eggplants, whole, for about 30 to 40 minutes, or until very tender.

Slice lengthwise and scoop the flesh into the bowl of a food processor. Add the olive oil, honey, and chili paste; pulse until the mixture is chopped fine. Serve as a spread for crostini or crackers, or stir into freshly cooked pasta.

2   medium eggplants

2   tablespoons olive oil

4   tablespoons honey

1   teaspoon hot chili paste, or
    1 teaspoon hot chili flakes

SERVES 8

SEARED FOIE GRAS
APPLE AND PEAR SLICES & HUCKLEBERRY-PORT SAUCE

THIS IS A SIGNATURE DISH AT THE STEPHANIE INN AND AN IDEAL APPETIZER FOR SPECIAL OCCASIONS. POUR A GLASS OF CHAMPAGNE, SAUTERNS, OR SWEET RIESLING TO HIGHLIGHT THE RICHNESS OF THE FOIE GRAS AND THE SWEET, TART FLAVORS OF THE HUCKLEBERRY SAUCE. FOIE GRAS CAN BE PURCHASED AT SPECIALTY BUTCHER SHOPS OR THROUGH MAIL-ORDER COMPANIES (LOOK FOR D'ARTAGNAN ON THE INTERNET). WHEN HUCKLEBERRIES ARE NOT IN SEASON, SUBSTITUTE OTHER SWEET FRUITS, SUCH AS FRESH BLUEBERRIES, BLACKBERRIES, OR CURRANTS.

APPLE AND PEAR SLICES

3   tablespoons butter

2   apples

2   pears

HUCKLEBERRY SAUCE

2   cups huckleberries
     (or blueberries)

1   cup port

4   tablespoons (1/2 stick) butter,
     chilled

Salt and freshly ground black pepper
     to taste

SEARED FOIE GRAS

8   ounces foie gras
     (fattened duck or, in
     Europe, goose liver)

2   tablespoons Calvados
     (apple brandy) or Cognac

Salt and freshly ground black pepper
     to taste

Chopped chives for garnish

SERVES 4

To prepare the Apple and Pear Slices: Melt 3 tablespoons of butter in a large skillet over medium heat. Leaving the peel intact, cut the apples and pears into 3/8-inch thick slices. You will need 4 large slices of each fruit. Remove the seeds from the center of each slice. Sauté the apple and pear slices in the warm butter, turning occasionally. Cook until just tender when pierced with a fork, about 5 minutes. Remove from the heat and set aside.

To prepare the Huckleberry-Port Sauce: Combine the huckleberries and port in a skillet. Bring to a boil over high heat; reduce to a low boil and cook until the sauce is thick and syrupy, about 10 to 15 minutes. Quickly whisk in the cold butter, a bit at a time. Season to taste with salt and pepper. Turn off the heat, and cover the sauce to keep it warm.

To prepare the Seared Foie Gras: Heat a skillet over high heat. Meanwhile, divide the foie gras into 4 portions and season with salt and pepper. When the pan is hot, add the foie gras and sear about 1 minute on each side, or until it is golden and just cooked through. Pour the Calvados into a ladle and light it with a match to flame. Pour the flaming Calvados over the foie gras, stirring gently until the flames are extinguished. Remove from the heat and set aside.

To assemble and serve: Place an apple slice in the center of each of 4 salad plates. Top with the foie gras, then add a pear slice. Ladle the huckleberry sauce over the top of the pear slice and around the apple slice. Garnish with chopped chives.

NORTHWEST MUSHROOMS: WILD TO EXOTIC

WITH ITS MILD, DAMP CLIMATE AND RICH WOODLAND SOILS, THE PACIFIC NORTHWEST IS A MUSHROOM COLLECTOR'S PARADISE. NEARLY EVERY MONTH OF THE YEAR, WITH FALL AND SPRING BEING THE PRIME MUSHROOMING SEASONS, THE FOREST FLOORS OF OREGON ERUPT WITH MUSHROOMS OF ALL SHAPES, COLORS AND SIZES. EDIBLE SPECIES INCLUDE OYSTER MUSHROOMS, GOLDEN CHANTERELLES, BOLETUS EDULIS (PORCINI), MORELS, GIANT PUFF BALLS, SHAGGY MANES, MATSUTAKE, HEN-OF-THE-WOODS, HEDGEHOG MUSHROOMS, GIANT CAULIFLOWER MUSHROOMS, CORAL MUSHROOMS AND MANY MORE. IN ADDITION TO THESE, MANY FLAVORFUL MUSHROOMS ARE NOW BEING CULTIVATED.

OYSTER MUSHROOM: Pale gray to beige, oyster mushrooms, often sprout on dead alder trees. They have a delicate woodsy flavor with distinct notes of anise. These delicate mushrooms, with their frilly, oyster-shell shaped cap, are both wild and cultivated.

PORCINI *(Boletus Edulis)* also known as cèpes: Porcinis, whose caps often reach up to eight or more inches across, are thick and meaty, with a creamy, earthy flavor. These golden-brown mushrooms have bulbous stems and big, round caps—the classic mushroom shape. They are harvested wild and sold fresh and dried.

CHANTERELLE: Wild golden chanterelles, with their delicate apricot scent, and sweet, earthy flavor, are a favorite with Northwest cooks. Shaped like an umbrella that's been folded inside-out, chanterelles are harvested wild in the spring and the fall. White and black chanterelles also grow wild in the Northwest. The black chanterelle is cultivated locally on a small scale.

MOREL: People often describe earth-brown, pinecone-shaped morels as looking "sponge-like" or "coral-like," due to their chambered outer flesh. Sweet and earthy, with a delicious caramel flavor when sautéed in butter or olive oil, morels are harvested wild each spring, and they may soon become available commercially. They are also sold dried.

CRIMINI: This is a cultivated, brown version of our white button mushroom, and is now available in most supermarkets. It has a heartier flavor than white button mushrooms, adding more taste when used as a substitute.

PORTOBELLO: This is a favorite of vegetarian chefs because of its thick "meaty" flesh, which can be grilled like a steak. Portobellos are cultivated mushrooms with dark brown gills and a cap that measures at least 4 1/4-inches wide and 1/2-inch thick.

ENOKI: Long, thin, and ivory-colored with tiny white caps, these cultivated mushrooms are often used as a garnish. Add them to dishes at the end of cooking for flavor and appearance.

SHIITAKE: Also known as Black Forest mushrooms, these flavorful mushrooms are used fresh and dried, especially in Asian cooking. The umbrella-shaped, rusty-brown cap sits atop a slender cream-colored stem, which is very tough and should be removed before cooking.

MATSUTAKE: Highly favored in Asian cooking, Matsutake mushrooms have a pungent, spicy aroma, similar to horseradish. They are harvested in the fall under Northwest pines. These brown-gilled mushrooms have a cream- to beige-colored cap and stem. The cap ranges from 3 to 5 inches in diameter.

SAFETY NOTE

While many wild mushrooms are safe to eat and very delicious, others can be highly toxic, or even deadly. It is crucial to properly identify all wild mushrooms. If you're not absolutely certain which species a mushroom is, don't eat it.

FOREST MUSHROOMS
BALSAMIC MARINADE

4   cups mushrooms

BALSAMIC MARINADE

1/2   cup balsamic vinegar

1   tablespoon soy sauce

2   garlic cloves, minced

1   tablespoon chopped chives

1   tablespoon chopped fresh
      parsley

1½   cups olive oil

1/2   cup water

1   tablespoon Dijon mustard

Salt and freshly ground pepper
      to taste

WHEN THE SEASON PERMITS, THE CHEFS OF THE STEPHANIE INN UTILIZE WILD FOREST MUSHROOMS (SUCH AS PORCINI, CHANTERELLES, OR MORELS) FOR THIS DISH. YOU CAN SUBSTITUTE BUTTON MUSHROOMS, OR ANY EXOTIC CULTIVATED MUSHROOMS. THE COOKED MUSHROOMS ARE EXCELLENT SERVED ON CRISP CROSTINI OR CRACKERS, OR SERVE THEM OVER ASIAN-STYLE NOODLES FOR A VEGETARIAN ENTRÉE.

Preheat the oven to 350° F.

Clean the mushrooms with a soft brush or damp sponge. Trim the ends from the mushroom stems and, if necessary, slice the mushrooms into bite-size pieces. Place the mushrooms in a large bowl and toss with the marinade. Turn the mushrooms into a baking dish and roast for 15 to 30 minutes, or until they are soft and cooked through. Season with salt and pepper.

To serve: Spread on crostini or crackers or serve over a bed of Asian noodles.

SERVES 6

Sautéed Mushroom Caps
Soy Sauce & Asiago Cheese

Serve these cheesy mushrooms as an appetizer, or as a side dish for meat, poultry, or seafood. They can be prepared ahead and placed under the broiler just before serving—broiling until the cheese is hot and melted.

Clean the mushrooms with a soft brush or damp sponge. Trim and discard the ends of the stems (or set aside for another use).

Heat the olive oil in a large skillet over medium-high heat. Add the garlic and shallots and cook for about 1 minute, or until the shallots are tender. Add the mushrooms and cook for about 2 minutes. Pour in the wine and soy sauce, and add the herbs; cook until the mushrooms are tender, adding more wine if needed.

Strain the mushrooms and place on an oven-proof serving platter. Season the mushrooms with salt and pepper and sprinkle liberally with grated cheese. If desired, place the mushrooms under a hot broiler to melt the cheese, about 1 minute.

20	medium button or crimini mushrooms
3	tablespoons olive oil
3	garlic cloves, minced
2	shallots, minced
2/3	cup dry white wine
2	tablespoons soy sauce
1	tablespoon finely sliced chives
1	tablespoon chopped fresh parsley

Salt and freshly ground black pepper

3/4 cup grated Asiago cheese

Serves 6

SEAFOOD STRUDEL

2 tablespoons olive oil

2 shallots, minced

2 garlic cloves, minced

4 cups seafood (such as salmon, halibut, sole, prawns or crab) skinned, deboned, and cut into 1/2-inch pieces

Juice and zest of 1 lemon

1 cup mascarpone cheese

1/4 cup chopped chives

1/4 cup chopped fresh parsley

2 tablespoons chopped fresh tarragon

6-8 layers phyllo dough

1/2 cup (1 stick) butter, melted

THIS RECIPE CALLS FOR FRESH FISH OF ANY KIND. USE SALMON, HALIBUT, OR TUNA, FOR EXAMPLE. YOU CAN ALSO ADD FRESHLY COOKED CRAB, SHRIMP, OR PRAWNS. IF YOU PREFER A VEGETARIAN DISH, SUBSTITUTE A VARIETY OF WILD OR CULTIVATED SAUTÉED MUSHROOMS FOR THE SEAFOOD. POUR A CRISP SAUVIGNON BLANC, DRY RIESLING, OR PINOT BLANC TO BRING OUT THE SEA-SWEET FLAVORS IN THIS DISH.

Heat the olive oil in a large skillet over medium heat. When the oil is hot, add the shallots and garlic and cook about 2 minutes, or until the shallots are soft and transparent. Add the seafood and cook, stirring often, until it is just cooked through, about 12 minutes. Turn the seafood mixture into a large mixing bowl. Gently fold in the lemon juice and zest, mascarpone cheese, chives, parsley and tarragon. Set the mixture aside to cool slightly.

Preheat the oven to 350° F.

Line a baking sheet with parchment paper or lightly brush it with cooking oil.

Working with 1 sheet of phyllo dough at a time, lay it out on a flat surface. Cover the remaining sheets of dough with plastic wrap or a damp kitchen towel to keep them from drying out. Brush the dough lightly with melted butter; add another layer of dough and brush with melted butter. Repeat until you have 6 layers of dough.

Starting 2 inches from the end of the layered phyllo dough, spread the prepared seafood mixture smoothly and horizontally across one end of the dough. Beginning at the end with the seafood mixture, tuck the short end of the dough over the filling, then roll into a tight roll. Tuck the ends of the phyllo dough underneath the roll. Place the roll on the prepared baking sheet. Brush the roll with the remaining melted butter and bake for about 35 minutes, or until golden. Let rest 5 minutes before slicing.

To serve: For appetizer portions, slice into 1-inch wide pieces. For entrée portions, slice into pieces 3 to 4 inches wide.

SERVES 8 AS AN APPETIZER OR 2 TO 4 AS AN ENTRÉE

Seared Scallops
Glazed Parsnips & Sautéed Wild Mushrooms

It is difficult to imagine a more magical, yet seemingly unlikely, combination of flavors, than sea-sweet scallops and earthy-sweet parsnips. Yet, somehow, the flavors blend beautifully and are further enhanced by the addition of wild mushrooms, with their own sweet, earthy flavors. The parsnips and wild mushrooms can be prepared up to 2 hours in advance and reheated just before serving. Cook the scallops at the last minute. A rich, buttery Chardonnay with tropical fruit flavors is a wonderful match with this dish.

To prepare the Glazed Parsnips: Heat the butter in a medium-sized skillet over medium-high heat. Stir in the parsnips, mixing well. Pour in the water, then lower the heat to a simmer and cook until the liquid is reduced and the parsnips are tender, about 15 minutes. Season to taste with salt and pepper and cover to keep warm.

To prepare the Sautéed Wild Mushrooms: Heat the butter and olive oil in a large skillet over medium heat. Add the garlic and wild mushrooms. Cook, stirring often, until the mushrooms are very tender, about 20 minutes. Add the wine and simmer until the mixture is reduced, about 5 minutes. Remove from the heat, set aside, and season with salt and pepper.

To prepare the Seared Scallops: Pat the scallops dry on paper towels. Meanwhile, heat the olive oil in a skillet over medium-high heat. Add the scallops and season with salt and pepper. Sear on each side until golden, about 1 minute per side, until the scallops are cooked through. Remove from the heat and set aside.

To serve: Place the wild mushrooms in the center of each plate. Spoon the parsnips around the mushrooms. Top the mushrooms with the seared scallops and their pan juices. Garnish with fresh parsley.

Glazed Parsnips

1 tablespoon butter

2 medium parsnips, peeled and sliced into 1/4-inch slices

1/2 cup water

Salt and freshly ground black pepper to taste

Sautéed Wild Mushrooms

2 tablespoons butter

1 tablespoon olive or canola oil

1 garlic clove, minced

1 shallot, minced

1 cup wild or cultivated exotic mushrooms, cleaned and quartered

2 tablespoons white wine

Salt and freshly ground black pepper to taste

Seared Scallops

8 large, fresh scallops

3 tablespoons olive oil

Salt and ground white pepper to taste

Fresh parsley leaves for garnish

Serves 4

ASIAGO CHIPS

8 ounces Asiago or Parmesan cheese, finely grated

Vegetable oil or non-stick spray

THESE CHEESY CHIPS ARE DELICIOUS WITH CHAMPAGNE AND SMOKED SALMON OR OYSTERS ON THE HALF SHELL.

Preheat the oven to 350° F.

Liberally grease a baking sheet with vegetable oil or non-stick spray.

Sprinkle the cheese evenly over the prepared baking sheet. Place the cheese in the oven and bake for about 8 to 12 minutes, or until the cheese is golden brown. Remove from the oven and let cool. Break into pieces.

SERVES 6

CREAMY CORN SOUP
DUNGENESS CRAB

3 tablespoons butter

3 tablespoons vegetable oil

2 medium white onions, diced

2 garlic cloves, minced

2 leeks (white part only), cleaned and diced

8 ears of corn

4 cups water

1 bay leaf

2 cups heavy cream

Salt and white pepper to taste

Tabasco sauce to taste

9 ounces fresh Dungeness crabmeat, picked through to remove shells

Hot red chili oil and chopped chives for garnish

DUNGENESS CRAB IS THE "KING OF CRABS" ON THE PACIFIC COAST. IT'S THE HIGHLIGHT OF THIS RICH SOUP MADE WITH FRESH, LOCALLY RAISED CORN. AFTER REMOVING AND RESERVING THE KERNELS, THE CHEFS SIMMER THE COBS WITH CHOPPED ONION AND A BAY LEAF TO MAKE A FLAVORFUL CORN STOCK. HOT RED CHILI OIL ADDS A LITTLE BITE TO THE FINISHED SOUP.

In a skillet, heat the butter with the oil over medium heat. Stir in the onions, garlic, and leeks. Cook on low heat, covered, for about 10 to 15 minutes, stirring occasionally, until the onions are very tender.

Meanwhile, slice the corn kernels from the cobs. Set the corn aside and reserve the cobs for the broth.

Pour the water into the onion mixture; add the bay leaf and the corncobs and bring the mixture to a boil. Reduce the heat to a simmer and cook for about 20 minutes. Remove and discard the cobs. Add the corn kernels and the cream, and simmer until the mixture is reduced by 1/3 (about 35 minutes). Working in batches, purée the soup in a blender or food processor; then pass the soup through a fine sieve. Reheat the soup over medium heat, stirring occasionally, until hot. Season with salt, white pepper, and Tabasco.

To serve: Ladle the soup into pre-warmed soup bowls. Distribute the crab evenly in the center of the bowls and garnish each bowl with chopped chives. Dot with red chili sauce around the edges.

SERVES 6

OYSTER STEW
LEMONGRASS

20	small oysters, shucked, reserving oyster liquor
2	tablespoons butter
2	garlic cloves, minced
2	shallots, minced
1/4	cup dry white wine
2	cups half-and-half
1½	cups heavy cream
1	stalk lemongrass, sliced in 3-inch pieces

Reserved oyster liquor

Fresh lemon juice to taste

Salt and white pepper to taste

2	tablespoons chopped chives for garnish

LOOK FOR SMALL OYSTERS, SUCH AS KUMAMOTOS (CRASSOSTREA SIKAMEA), FOR THIS RECIPE. IF THEY ARE NOT AVAILABLE, BUY THE FRESHEST, MOST FLAVORFUL OYSTERS YOU CAN FIND AND SLICE THEM INTO BITE-SIZE PIECES. A GREAT MAIL-ORDER SOURCE FOR KUMAMOTO OYSTERS IS TAYLOR SHELLFISH FARMS, LOCATED IN SHELTON, WASHINGTON. WARM SOURDOUGH BREAD AND A CRISP WHITE WINE MAKE GREAT ACCOMPANIMENTS.

Shuck the oysters and strain the liquor into a separate bowl. Set the oysters aside.

Melt the butter in a soup kettle over medium heat. Stir in the garlic and shallots; cook until the shallots are tender, about 7 minutes. Stir in the wine, half-and-half, cream, lemon grass, and reserved oyster liquor. Reduce the heat to a simmer and cook the soup for about 30 minutes, stirring occasionally. Using a slotted spoon, remove the lemon grass.

Add the oysters and cook about 2 minutes, just until the edges curl. Season the soup with lemon juice, salt and white pepper.

To serve: Ladle into pre-warmed soup bowls and garnish with chopped chives.

SERVES 4

Yukon Gold Potato-Leek Soup

GOLDEN-FLESHED, LOCALLY RAISED YUKON GOLD POTATOES ARE DELICIOUS IN THIS CREAMY SOUP. YOU CAN ALSO USE NEW RED POTATOES.

In a soup kettle, sauté the bacon over medium heat until crisp. Drain it on paper towels and set aside. Pour the bacon grease out of the kettle. Put the butter into the kettle and, when it is melted, add the onion, leeks, and minced garlic. Cook, stirring often, until the onions are soft and translucent. Stir in the diced potatoes and cover with the water (adding more water if necessary to cover). Cook until the potatoes are tender when pierced with a fork. Purée half of the potato mixture in a food processor; then stir the purée back into the other potatoes. Stir in the heavy cream and season to taste with fresh lemon juice, salt, and pepper.

To serve: Ladle into pre-warmed soup bowls. Garnish with chopped chives and bacon.

4	slices bacon, cut into 1/2-inch pieces
2	tablespoons butter
1	medium sweet onion (such as Walla Walla, Texas Sweet, or Mayan), diced
4	leeks (white part only), rinsed and thinly sliced
2	garlic cloves, minced
4	pounds unpeeled Yukon gold potatoes, rinsed and diced
2	cups water, approximate
2	cups heavy cream

Fresh lemon juice to taste

Salt and freshly ground black pepper to taste

Chopped chives for garnish

SERVES 4

Tuscan White Bean Soup

8   ounces dry white kidney beans, soaked overnight

8   cups water, unsalted

1/4 cup olive oil

3   ounces pancetta or bacon, diced

1   medium onion, diced

4   garlic cloves, minced

2   leeks, rinsed and finely sliced

4   ounces celery root (or celery), finely diced

4   medium tomatoes, cored and diced

2   cups shredded Savoy cabbage

Salt and freshly ground black pepper to taste

1   cup chicken or vegetable broth, preferably homemade

1   sprig fresh rosemary

1   sprig fresh thyme

2   bay leaves

Pesto for garnish (see Recipe Index)

Serves 4

Nothing tastes better on a cold, blustery day at the beach than a bowl of hot bean soup loaded with fresh vegetables and diced pancetta. Serve this tasty soup with slices of homemade bread and a glass of Pinot Noir or Chianti.

Put the beans in a large kettle and cover with water. Soak overnight. Drain the soaking water from the beans and add 8 cups water, adding more water as necessary to keep the beans covered during cooking. Bring the beans to a boil, then reduce the heat and simmer until they are soft, stirring occasionally, about 1 hour. Purée one-half of the beans in a food processor or blender and stir back into the whole beans.

Cook pancetta separately until crispy. Reserve.

Heat the olive oil in a large skillet over medium-high heat. Add the onion, garlic, leeks, celery root, tomatoes, and cabbage. Cook, stirring often, until the vegetables are tender, about 12 minutes. Add the vegetables to the beans and season to taste with salt and pepper. Bring the soup to a boil, and then reduce the heat to a simmer.

In a separate saucepan, bring the beef broth to a boil with the rosemary, thyme, and bay leaves. Remove from the heat and let the herbs steep for 5 to 10 minutes. Strain the herbs from the broth and stir the broth into the soup.

To serve: Ladle into pre-warmed soup bowls and garnish each bowl with 1 teaspoon of pesto and 1/4 of the cooked pancetta.

Pacific Coast Seafood Chowder

Teeming with fresh seafood, including prawns, salmon, halibut, and clams, the majestic Pacific Ocean provides an incredible array of ingredients for the chefs at The Stephanie Inn. Served with warm garlic bread or sourdough bread and a glass of light red wine, this soul-warming chowder is guaranteed to warm your bones on a cold winter day. You can substitute any fresh, firm fish from your local seafood purveyor (such as black cod, tuna or swordfish). Mussels and scallops in the shell are also welcome additions.

Preheat the oven to 300° F.

Toss the tomatoes lightly in olive oil and sprinkle with salt and pepper. Place in an ovenproof glass baking dish and roast for about 40 minutes, or until soft.

Melt the butter and oil together in a large soup kettle over medium heat. Stir in the onion, garlic, thyme, and oregano; cook for about 5 minutes, or until the onions are tender. Stir in the white wine, fish stock, and diced potatoes. Simmer until the potatoes are tender, about 15 to 20 minutes.

With the broth still simmering, add the salmon and halibut and cook about 10 minutes, stirring gently, until the fish is firm and almost cooked through. Add the prawns and clams and cover the pan. Cook 7 to 10 more minutes, or until the prawns are bright pink and the clams have opened. Stir in the heavy cream.

To serve: Ladle the chowder into pre-warmed bowls and sprinkle with chopped parsley or chives to garnish.

6	medium tomatoes
1	tablespoon olive oil
Salt and freshly ground pepper to taste	
2	tablespoons butter
2	tablespoons olive or canola oil
1	medium white onion, diced
3	garlic cloves, minced
1	teaspoon thyme
1	cup dry white wine
2	cups fish stock (see Recipe Index)
2	medium new potatoes, rinsed and diced (peels intact)
6	ounces fresh salmon, skinned, deboned, and diced
6	ounces fresh halibut, skinned, deboned, and diced
8	prawns, shelled and deveined
20	small steamer clams, rinsed
1½	cups heavy cream
Salt and freshly ground black pepper to taste	

Fresh chopped parsley or chives for garnish

Serves 4

CURRIED CARROT SOUP
SOUR CREAM & CHIVES

2   tablespoons butter

2   tablespoons vegetable oil

1   medium onion, diced

1   leek (white part only), diced

6   medium carrots, sliced

3   tablespoons grated fresh ginger

2   garlic cloves, minced

2   teaspoons red curry paste,
      or to taste

4   cups vegetable stock (see
      Recipe Index) or water

1   cup heavy cream

Juice of 1/2 lemon, or to taste

Salt and freshly ground black pepper
      to taste

Sour cream, grated ginger, and
      chopped chives for garnish

FRESH GINGER, A TOUCH OF RED CURRY, AND SWIRL OF SOUR CREAM MAKE FOR A PERFECT, TASTY BLEND IN THIS SIMPLE SOUP, GOOD ANY TIME OF THE YEAR.

In a large soup kettle, melt the butter with the oil over medium heat. Stir in the onion, leek, and carrots. Cover and cook, stirring occasionally, until the vegetables are tender, about 8 to 10 minutes. Stir in the ginger, garlic, and curry paste. Add the water and the cream, and bring the soup to a boil. Working in several batches, purée the soup in a food processor or blender. Press through a strainer, and then reheat just before serving. Season with lemon juice and salt and pepper to taste.

To serve: Ladle the soup into pre-warmed soup bowls. Add a tablespoonful of sour cream to each bowl and swirl the sour cream with a knife. Sprinkle each bowl with grated ginger and chopped chives.

SERVES 4

Roasted Garlic & Potato Soup

THICK AND EARTHY, THIS SOUP IS PERFECT FOR A CHILLY AUTUMN DAY. A GLASS OF AN ELEGANT, FRUITY PINOT NOIR IS THE ULTIMATE ACCOMPANIMENT.

Preheat the oven to 325° F.

Toss the garlic and olive oil together in a small baking dish and roast until soft, about 30 to 40 minutes. Remove the garlic from the oven and set aside.

Meanwhile, melt the butter in a skillet over medium heat. Stir in the onion and thyme. Reduce the heat to low. Cover and cook until the onions are very soft, about 15 minutes. Stir in the diced potatoes. Add the water and cream. Bring to a simmer and cook until the potatoes are tender, about 20 minutes. Add the roasted garlic.

Purée the mixture in a blender or food processor, working in batches if necessary, and adding more cream to reach the desired consistency. Reheat the soup on the stove. Season to taste with with fresh lemon juice, salt, and pepper.

To serve: Ladle the soup into pre-warmed soup bowls and garnish with fresh thyme leaves.

12	garlic cloves, peeled and ends trimmed
1	tablespoon olive oil
1/4	cup (1/2 stick) butter
1	large onion, diced
3	sprigs fresh thyme, stems removed
4	large, unpeeled red or yellow new potatoes, diced
3	cups water
3	cups heavy cream
	Salt and freshly ground black pepper to taste
	Freshly squeezed lemon juice to taste
	Fresh thyme leaves for garnish

SERVES 6 TO 8

ROASTED FENNEL SOUP

6   bulbs fresh fennel, thinly sliced
      (reserve greens for garnish)

3   tablespoons olive oil

4   tablespoons (1/2 stick) butter

2   medium onions, diced

2   stalks celery, chopped

4   garlic cloves, minced

3   sprigs fresh thyme, stems
      removed

3   cups heavy cream

3   cups water

Salt and freshly ground black pepper
      to taste

Sour cream and fennel sprigs for
      garnish

IF YOU HAVE NEVER TASTED ROASTED, LICORICE-FLAVORED FENNEL BULBS, YOU ARE IN FOR A DELIGHTFUL SURPRISE. ROASTING BRINGS OUT A SWEET, ANISE-FLAVORED EARTHINESS THAT NO OTHER VEGETABLE CAN ATTAIN. SERVE THIS WARM IN THE WINTER OR CHILLED FOR A REFRESHING SUMMER SOUP.

Preheat the oven to 350° F.

Combine the sliced fennel and olive oil in a baking pan and bake for about 40 minutes, until the fennel is very tender.

Meanwhile, melt the butter in a large soup kettle. Stir in the onions, celery, garlic, and thyme. Cook, stirring occasionally, until the onions are soft. Stir in the roasted fennel, cream, and water. Let the mixture simmer for about 25 minutes to marry the flavors.

Working in batches, as necessary, purée the soup in a blender or food processor and strain through a fine sieve. Season to taste with salt and pepper.

To serve: Ladle into warm soup bowls and garnish with sour cream and fennel sprigs. Or, chill first to serve cold on a hot summer day.

SERVES 6 TO 8

CARAMELIZED SWEET ONION SOUP

GROWN IN EASTERN WASHINGTON, WALLA WALLA SWEET ONIONS ARE PRIZED THROUGHOUT THE NORTHWEST AND BEYOND. OTHER ONIONS CAN BE SUBSTITUTED, SUCH AS TEXAS OR MAUI SWEETS. THE CHEFS AT THE STEPHANIE INN RECOMMEND A GARNISH OF CRISPY FRIED ONIONS (SEE RECIPE BELOW).

To prepare the Caramelized Sweet Onion Soup: In a large soup kettle, melt the butter over high heat. Add the onions, garlic, thyme, and bay leaves. Cook, without stirring, until the onions begin to caramelize (they should be golden throughout with some dark brown edges). Continue to cook and stir the onions until they are dark golden throughout. Stir in the cream and water and season to taste with salt and pepper. Reduce the heat and simmer until the soup is slightly reduced, about 20 minutes. Remove the bay leaves. Add more salt and pepper and fresh lemon juice to taste.

To make the Crispy Fried Onions: In a mixing bowl, toss together the onion, flour, salt, and pepper. Add vegetable oil to a large skillet, adding enough to make it 2 inches deep. Heat over a medium-high heat until the oil reaches 350° F. Drop in the onion slices and fry until crispy. Remove with a slotted spoon and drain on paper towels.

To serve: Ladle into pre-warmed soup bowls and garnish with Crispy Fried Onions.

CARAMELIZED SWEET ONION SOUP

4	tablespoons (1/2 stick) butter
6	large Walla Walla Sweet onions, peeled and thinly sliced
2	garlic cloves, minced
4	sprigs fresh thyme, stems removed
2	bay leaves
2	cups heavy cream
4	cups water

Salt and freshly ground black pepper to taste

Freshly squeezed lemon juice to taste

CRISPY FRIED ONIONS

1	large onion, peeled and very thinly sliced into long pieces
1/2	cup all-purpose flour
2	teaspoons salt
1	teaspoon freshly ground black pepper
1	cup vegetable oil, approximately, to fill skillet 2" deep

SERVES 6 TO 8

SPRING ASPARAGUS SOUP

2   tablespoons butter

2   tablespoons canola or
     safflower oil

1   white onion, peeled and diced

1   leek (white part only), sliced

2   garlic cloves, minced

2   bunches fresh asparagus,
     rinsed and ends trimmed
     (approximately 2 pounds)

2   sprigs fresh thyme

2   cups chicken stock

2   cups heavy cream

Salt and ground white pepper
     to taste

Freshly squeezed lemon juice
     to taste

1/4 cup sour cream

4   shiitake mushrooms,
     thinly sliced and sautéed in
     2 tablespoons butter

1/4 cup finely chopped chives

Reserved asparagus

4 thin slices of crisply fried bacon

SERVES 4

THIS CREAMY ASPARAGUS SOUP IS GARNISHED WITH SOUR CREAM, SAUTÉED SHIITAKE MUSHROOMS, CHOPPED CHIVES, AND A SLENDER CURL OF CRISP BACON. DELICIOUS!

Heat the butter and oil in a heavy-bottomed soup kettle over medium heat. Stir in the onion, leek, and minced garlic. Cook, stirring often, until the vegetables are tender, about 10 minutes. Set aside 4 whole stalks of asparagus. Cut the remaining asparagus into 1-inch pieces. Add the cut and whole asparagus stalks to the kettle and sauté, stirring gently, until it is tender. Remove the whole stalks of asparagus and set aside to cool. When the stalks are cool enough to handle, slice each one in half lengthwise.

Add the thyme sprigs, chicken stock, and cream to the vegetables in the pan. Bring the mixture to a boil, then reduce the heat and simmer for about 20 minutes. Remove the thyme and purée the soup in a food processor or blender. If desired, strain the purée through a fine sieve for a silkier texture. Season to taste with salt, pepper and lemon juice.

To serve: Ladle the soup into pre-warmed soup bowls. Top each serving with a tablespoon of sour cream, sautéed mushrooms, a sprinkle of chopped chives, 2 halves of the reserved sautéed asparagus spears, and a slice of crisp bacon.

ROASTED TOMATO SOUP
PRAWNS & BASIL

12   Roma tomatoes, or small red
      tomatoes, cut in half

1/4   cup olive oil

2   garlic cloves, minced

1   teaspoon dried oregano

1   teaspoon dried parsley

Salt and freshly ground black pepper
      to taste

2   tablespoons butter or
      vegetable oil

1   onion, peeled and diced

1   leek (white part only),
      rinsed and sliced

2   garlic cloves, minced

16   large fresh prawns, shelled,
      deveined and tails removed

1/2   cup dry white wine

2   cups water

Salt and freshly ground black pepper
      to taste

Chopped fresh basil for garnish

SERVES 4

ROASTING THE TOMATOES FIRST WITH OIL AND HERBS CREATES A TOMATO SOUP WITH A DEPTH AND FLAVOR NOT FOUND IN THE VERSION YOU RECALL FROM CHILDHOOD.

Preheat the oven to 350° F.

Place the tomatoes halves, garlic, salt, pepper, olive oil, and herbs in a baking pan and mix well. Roast until the tomatoes are very soft and have started to brown on the edges, about 1 hour.

When the tomatoes are cool enough to handle, purée them in a blender or food processor and set them aside. (These can be prepared up to 4 hours in advance.)

Meanwhile, melt the butter in a skillet over medium heat and stir in the onions, leek, minced garlic, and thyme. Cook, stirring often, until the vegetables are soft, about 10 minutes. Stir in the prawns and cook for about 5 minutes, until they begin to turn red. Remove 8 prawns and set aside for the garnish. Stir in the white wine and water and simmer for about 15 minutes. Stir in the tomato purée and simmer until the soup is heated through. Season to taste with salt, pepper, and cayenne pepper.

To serve: Ladle soup into pre-warmed soup bowls and garnish with the reserved prawns and chopped basil.

Fresh Tomato & Herb Soup

IN CONTRAST WITH THE DEEP FLAVORS GAINED BY THE LONG ROASTING OF TOMATOES IN THE RECIPE ON THE PREVIOUS PAGE, THIS ONE CELEBRATES FRESH-FROM-THE-GARDEN FLAVOR.

Heat the olive oil in a soup kettle over medium heat. Stir in the garlic and shallots. Cover and cook for about 8 minutes, or until the shallots are tender and opaque. Stir in the diced tomatoes, parsley, and tomato juice. Simmer the soup for about 20 minutes, stirring occasionally. Add the basil and green onions, and simmer for about 10 minutes. Purée the soup in a food processor or blender. Pour the puréed soup back into the soup kettle. Add the heavy cream and season to taste with salt and pepper.

To serve: Ladle the soup into pre-warmed soup bowls and garnish with freshly chopped herbs.

1/4	cup olive oil
1	garlic clove, minced
2	shallots, minced
4	large vine-ripened tomatoes, diced
1/4	cup chopped fresh parsley
4	cups tomato juice
1/4	cup chopped fresh basil
1/2	cup sliced green onions
1/2	cup heavy cream

Salt and freshly ground black pepper to taste

Freshly chopped herbs for garnish

SERVES 4

FOREST MUSHROOM SOUP

8 tablespoons butter (1 stick)

2 large onions, diced

3 garlic cloves, minced

1 pound assorted wild mushrooms, wiped clean with a
damp cloth and stems trimmed

1 cup dry white wine

1/2 cup soy sauce

2 cups chicken stock or water

2 cups heavy cream

1/4 cup chopped fresh parsley

Salt and freshly ground black pepper
to taste

1/2 cup finely sliced shiitake or
crimini mushrooms sautéed
in olive oil until crisp for
garnish

DURING THE COOL, DAMP MONTHS OF SPRING AND FALL, THE OREGON COAST IS BLESSED WITH AN ARRAY OF FLAVORFUL WILD MUSHROOMS, INCLUDING CHANTERELLES, MORELS, PORCINI, AND OYSTER MUSHROOMS. THE STEPHANIE INN CHEFS ARE ALWAYS DELIGHTED WHEN THEIR FAVORITE MUSHROOM FORAGER, VERONICA WILLIAMS, STOPS BY WITH A BASKET OF JUST-PICKED WILD MUSHROOMS. WHEN WILD MUSHROOMS ARE NOT AVAILABLE, SUBSTITUTE CULTIVATED MUSHROOMS, SUCH AS SHIITAKE, OYSTER, PORTOBELLO, OR BUTTON MUSHROOMS. POUR A GLASS OF PINOT NOIR TO HIGHLIGHT THE SUBTLE EARTHY FLAVORS OF THIS SOUP.

Melt the butter in a large soup kettle over medium-high heat. Stir in the diced onions, and garlic and sauté for about 5 minutes, or until the onions are translucent. Add the mushrooms. Lower the heat to medium and cook, stirring often, until the mushrooms begin to soften, about 10 minutes. Stir in the white wine, and simmer for about 5 minutes; then add the soy sauce, stock or water, cream, and chopped parsley. Bring the soup to a boil, then reduce the heat and simmer for about 20 minutes. Season to taste with salt and pepper.

To serve: Ladle into pre-warmed soup bowls and garnish with crisp fried mushrooms.

SERVES 4

BALSAMIC VINAIGRETTE
Makes about 1 cup

4	tablespoons balsamic vinegar
1	garlic clove, minced
1	teaspoon sugar
3/4	cup olive oil
1	teaspoon Dijon mustard
2	teaspoons chopped fresh basil
2	teaspoons chopped chives

Salt and freshly ground black pepper
to taste

SALAD

2 to 3 large daikon radishes
(about 10 inches long)

Olive oil

2	cups mixed baby organic greens, such as spinach, lettuce, radicchio and Swiss chard
1	medium carrot, peeled and thinly sliced
2	cherry tomatoes, cut in half
1/4	cup Gorgonzola cheese, crumbled
1/4	cup chopped, toasted hazelnuts or pine nuts

Salt and freshly ground black pepper
to taste

Optional garnish: Small diamonds
cut from red and yellow peppers

ORGANIC GREENS
DAIKON RADISH, HAZELNUTS, GORGONZOLA & BALSAMIC VINAIGRETTE

THIN SLICES OF DAIKON (JAPANESE) RADISH LINE A MOLD TO CREATE A DRAMATIC HOLDER FOR THE GREENS IN THIS EYE-APPEALING SALAD. FOR A SIMPLER VERSION, FAN THE SLICED DAIKON ON A PLATE AND TOP WITH THE FRESH GREENS AND VEGETABLES. DAIKON IS A LONG, SLENDER WHITE RADISH THAT CAN BE PURCHASED AT MOST SUPERMARKETS.

To make the Balsamic Vinaigrette: Whisk all the ingredients together in a non-reactive bowl. Whisk again just before serving.

You can prepare this dressing up to 2 hours in advance, then cover and allow to sit at room temperature. Leftover dressing can be stored in the refrigerator for up to 4 days. Warm to room temperature and whisk before serving.

To prepare the salad: Lightly oil four 3-inch molds. Peel the daikon radish and slice into 1/8-inch thick rounds. Lightly brush both sides of each slice with olive oil. Line the molds with the radish slices, overlapping them slightly, to form a circular crown on the inner sides of each mold (see photo).

Place half of the baby greens in the center of each mold; top with sliced carrots, cherry tomato slices and crumbled Gorgonzola cheese.

To serve: Unmold the salads by gently pulling the molds up and over the salad, as though pulling your arm out of a coat sleeve. Spoon the Balsamic Vinaigrette over the top of the salads and sprinkle with chopped, toasted hazelnuts. Season with salt and pepper to taste.

Garnish with small diamonds cut from red and yellow peppers if desired.

CHEF'S TIP

At The Stephanie Inn, the chefs mold this colorful salad in a 2-inch-high round of PVC pipe. A well-rinsed tuna fish can with the lid and bottom removed is a good substitute.

SERVES 2

ROASTED TOMATOES

2   large tomatoes, sliced

Olive oil

Salt and freshly ground black pepper
    to taste

APPLE CIDER
VINAIGRETTE

Makes about 3/4 cup

1/2   cup apple juice

1/4   cup canola or safflower oil

1/4   cup apple cider vinegar

1/2   teaspoon salt

1/2   teaspoon white pepper

2   teaspoons sugar

1   teaspoon lemon juice

BELGIAN ENDIVE AND
APPLE SALAD

3   heads Belgian endive, leaves
    separated, rinsed and dried

1   large crisp apple, such as
    Granny Smith, Fuji, Braeburn
    or Golden Delicious, peeled
    and julienned (soak in 2 table-
    spoons lemon juice to prevent
    browning)

1   stalk celery, julienned

SERVES 4

BELGIAN ENDIVE & APPLE SALAD
ROASTED TOMATOES & APPLE CIDER VINAIGRETTE

BELGIAN ENDIVE, A MEMBER OF THE CHICORY FAMILY, HAS LONG, TAPERED, PALE GREEN LEAVES WITH A CRISP TEXTURE AND A SLIGHTLY BITTER FLAVOR THAT BLENDS DELICIOUSLY WITH THE SWEET FLAVOR OF A FRESH APPLE AND THE TANG OF ROASTED TOMATOES.

To prepare the Roasted Tomatoes: Preheat the oven to 300° F. Toss the sliced tomatoes lightly in olive oil and sprinkle with salt and pepper; place in a glass pie plate and roast for about 8 to 10 minutes, or until soft. Set aside.

To make the Apple Cider Vinaigrette: Place the apple juice in a blender or food processor. Gradually add the canola oil, until it is well blended. Add the vinegar, salt, white pepper, sugar, and lemon juice, mixing well. Serve at room temperature.

To assemble and serve the salad: Arrange the tomato slices on four salad plates. Toss the endive in the vinaigrette and fan over the tomatoes. Top with the julienned apple and julienned celery.

STUFFED TOMATO
SPINACH & GOAT CHEESE

FILLED WITH A CREAMY MIXTURE OF GOAT CHEESE, HERBS AND SPINACH, THIS SALAD IS OUTSTANDING DURING THE SUMMER AND EARLY FALL WHEN PLUMP LUSCIOUS TOMATOES CAN BE PICKED RIGHT FROM THE VINE. SERVED ON A BED OF CRISP GREENS, THE TOMATOES MAKE AN EXCELLENT VEGETARIAN ENTRÉE OR A SIDE DISH FOR BEEF OR LAMB.

Heat the olive oil in a skillet over medium heat. Stir in the spinach and cook about 5 minutes, just until the spinach is tender. Season with salt and pepper and set aside.

Slice the tops off the tomatoes about 1/2-inch down, so that you have an opening large enough to fill. If necessary slice a tiny bit off the bottom of the tomatoes so that they will sit level on a plate. Using a small spoon, hollow out the center of the tomatoes. (If desired, reserve the pulp to use in a tomato sauce.) Blend together the goat cheese, Boursin cheese, and chives, and mix well. Pipe or spoon the cheese into the prepared tomatoes. Using a spoon handle, make a hole in the center of the cheese and stuff with the wilted spinach. Chill for 30 minutes to 4 hours.

To serve: Toss the fresh greens with Balsamic Vinaigrette. Divide the greens among four salad plates and top each plate with a stuffed tomato. Garnish with pine nuts and chopped chives.

1	tablespoon olive oil
3	cups fresh spinach, chopped
Salt and freshly ground black pepper to taste	
4	medium ripe, red tomatoes
1/2	cup soft goat cheese (about 5½ ounces), room temperature
1/4	cup herbed Boursin cheese, room temperature
3	tablespoons chopped chives
4	cups fresh salad greens, rinsed and dried

Balsamic Vinaigrette
(see Recipe Index)

1/2	cup pine nuts, toasted and chopped, for garnish
Chopped chives for garnish	

SERVES 4

CHILLED PRAWN AND VEGETABLE SALAD

2   tablespoons olive oil

1   garlic clove, minced

1   shallot, minced

10 large prawns, shelled and deveined (tails intact)

2   tablespoons finely chopped fresh parsley

3   tablespoons dry white wine

2   cups fresh baby greens, rinsed and dried

1   large tomato, sliced

1   small carrot, julienned

1/2 red onion, finely sliced

PESTO VINAIGRETTE

Makes about 1 cup

Juice of 1 lemon

1   teaspoon sugar

1   tablespoon white wine vinegar

1/2 cup olive oil

1   tablespoon Pesto (see Recipe Index)

SERVES 2 AS AN ENTRÉE

CHILLED PRAWN & VEGETABLE SALAD
PESTO VINAIGRETTE

SERVE THIS SALAD WITH WARM SOURDOUGH BREAD AND A CRISP WHITE WINE, SUCH AS A PINOT GRIS OR SAUVIGNON BLANC, FOR A DELICIOUS APPETIZER OR A LIGHT SUMMER ENTRÉE.

Heat the olive oil in a skillet over medium heat. When the oil is hot, stir in the minced garlic and shallots and sauté for 1 minute. Add the prawns, parsley, and white wine. Cook about 5 minutes, or until the prawns turn pink and are cooked through. Drain and discard the liquid and set the prawns aside to cool slightly.

Meanwhile, to prepare the Pesto Vinaigrette: In a non-reactive salad bowl, combine the lemon juice, sugar, vinegar, olive oil and pesto. Whisk until all ingredients are well blended. Toss the salad greens with the dressing.

To assemble and serve: Distribute the greens on two salad plates. Arrange the tomato slices around the edges of the greens, and place a prawn on top of each tomato. Garnish the salads with the julienned carrot and red onion slices and drizzle with more dressing.

12   cherry tomatoes

1-2   tablespoons olive oil

Salt and freshly ground black pepper
      to taste

WARM BACON DRESSING

6   slices bacon, diced

1/4   cup red wine vinegar

1/2   cup olive oil

1   teaspoon Dijon mustard

1/2   teaspoon mustard seed

2   tablespoons sugar

Salt and freshly ground black pepper
      to taste

6   cups fresh spinach,
      rinsed and dried

1/2   cup jicama, peeled and diced

SERVES 4

SPINACH SALAD
ROASTED TOMATOES, JICAMA & WARM BACON DRESSING

ROASTING THE CHERRY TOMATOES FOR THIS SALAD BRINGS OUT AN INCREDIBLY SWEET FLAVOR THAT PAIRS NICELY WITH THE TANGY DRESSING AND SALTY BACON. (THE TOMATOES CAN BE PREPARED UP TO 4 HOURS IN ADVANCE.) SERVED WITH FRESH BREAD AND A GLASS OF LIGHT RED WINE, SUCH AS A PINOT NOIR OR CHIANTI, THIS ALSO MAKES A DELICIOUS ENTRÉE FOR LUNCH OR DINNER.

Preheat the oven to 300° F.

Toss the cherry tomatoes lightly in olive oil and sprinkle with salt and pepper. Place in a glass pie plate and roast for about 30 minutes, or until soft.

To make the dressing: Meanwhile, cook the diced bacon in a large skillet over medium-high heat until crisp. Remove the bacon with a slotted spoon and drain on paper towels. Reserve 2 tablespoons of the bacon grease. Keep the bacon warm in a low oven. Meanwhile, whisk the vinegar, olive oil, mustard, mustard seed, and sugar into the reserved bacon grease and mix well. Stir in half of the cooked bacon and season to taste with salt and pepper.

To assemble and serve: Tear the spinach into bite-size pieces (if necessary) and toss with the warm dressing. Distribute the spinach over four salad plates. Top with the roasted tomatoes, diced jicama and the remaining bacon.

ROASTED BEET SALAD
HONEY-ORANGE DRESSING

EVEN IF YOU THINK YOU DON'T LIKE BEETS, CHANCES ARE YOU WILL LOVE THIS COLORFUL SALAD. SWEET ROASTED BEETS, ORANGES, JICAMA, AND FRESH GREENS ARE DRESSED IN A CITRUSY HONEY-ORANGE DRESSING. AT THE INN, THE CHEFS USE A JUICER TO MAKE FRESH BEET JUICE FOR THE DRESSING. YOU CAN ALSO FIND BOTTLED BEET JUICE AT SPECIALTY FOOD STORES.

To prepare the roasted beets: Preheat the oven to 350° F. Rub two beets with olive oil and wrap in foil. Roast for about 1 hour, or until cooked through. Remove from the oven, unwrap, and set aside until cool enough to handle. Peel beets and slice into thin rounds. Set aside.

To make the Honey-Orange Dressing: Peel the other two beets and process through a juicer (or use bottled beet juice). Combine the beet juice with the orange juice, vinegar, and honey, mixing well. Gradually whisk in the olive oil, whisking until thoroughly mixed. Season to taste with salt and pepper.

To assemble and serve: Toss the salad greens with the dressing and distribute among four salad plates. Layer the beet slices and orange segments around the salad and garnish with diced jicama.

2   large beets, ends trimmed

2   tablespoons olive oil

1 to 2 oranges, segmented

1   cup julienned jicama

1 to 2 heads red leaf lettuce, rinsed and dried

HONEY-ORANGE DRESSING

Makes about 2 cups

Juice of 2 beets or 1/4 cup bottled beet juice

1/4   cup orange juice

1/4   cup Champagne wine vinegar

1   tablespoon honey

1¼   cups olive oil

Salt and freshly ground pepper to taste

SERVES 4 TO 6

4 to 6 cooked duck breasts
(see Recipe Index for
Crispy Duck Breasts)

ORANGE SYRUP

1   cup orange juice (without pulp)

2   tablespoons honey

HONEY-LEMON DRESSING
Makes 1 1/2 cups

1/4   cup freshly squeezed
lemon juice

2   tablespoons honey

1/2   teaspoon lemon zest

2   tablespoons cold water

1   cup olive oil

Salt and freshly ground white
pepper to taste

2   tablespoons finely
chopped chives

SALAD

6   cups fresh baby greens, such as
spinach, butter lettuce, red leaf
lettuce and radicchio, rinsed
and dried

2   carrots, julienned or grated

1   daikon radish, julienned or
grated

SERVES 4 TO 6

DUCK BREAST SALAD
ORANGE SYRUP & HONEY-LEMON DRESSING

NOTHING COMPLEMENTS THE RICH FLAVOR OF DUCK BETTER THAN TART CITRUS-FLAVORED SAUCES AND FRESH LEAFY GREENS. PREPARE THE DUCK BREASTS ACCORDING TO THE RECIPE FOR CRISPY DUCK BREASTS (SEE RECIPE INDEX).

To prepare the Duck Breasts: Prepare the duck breasts following the recipe for Crispy Duck Breasts (see Recipe Index). Remove them from the heat and set aside to cool.

To make the Orange Syrup: Meanwhile, combine the orange juice and honey in a saucepan and bring to a boil over medium heat. Reduce the heat to low and simmer for about 12 to 15 minutes, or until the mixture becomes thick and syrupy. Set aside.

To prepare the Honey-Lemon Dressing: In a blender or food processor combine the lemon juice, honey, lemon zest, and water. Purée the ingredients, then gradually add the olive oil and blend until the dressing is thick and creamy. Transfer the dressing to a salad bowl; season with salt and pepper and fold in the chives.

To assemble and serve: Toss the greens with the Honey-Lemon Dressing and place on salad plates. Slice the duck breasts into 1/2-inch thick slices and fan out over the greens. Top the salad with the carrot and daikon radish. Drizzle the orange syrup around the edges of the plate and over the top of the salad.

PETRALE SOLE FILLETS
MASCARPONE CHEESE & HERBS

FILLED WITH A RICH BLEND OF MASCARPONE CHEESE AND FRESH HERBS, TENDER FILLETS OF SOLE ARE BAKED WITH LEMON JUICE AND WHITE WINE. SERVE WITH GARLIC-MASHED POTATOES (SEE RECIPE INDEX) AND A FRESH SALAD OR SAUTÉED VEGETABLES, AND POUR A BUTTERY CHARDONNAY OR OAK-AGED PINOT GRIS TO ACCENT THE FLAVORS IN THIS DISH.

4	6-ounce petrale sole fillets (or other flat white fish-fillets), skinned and deboned
1/2	cup (4 ounces) mascarpone cheese (or whipped cream cheese)
2	tablespoons chopped chives
2	tablespoons chopped fresh parsley
2	garlic cloves, minced
1	shallot, minced

Salt and freshly ground black pepper to taste

Vegetable oil as needed for oiling baking sheet

Juice of 1 lemon

1	cup dry white wine
1/2	cup water
1	tablespoon sugar
2	tablespoons butter, chilled and cut into 1/2-inch pieces

Lemon wedges and fresh herbs for garnish

SERVES 4

Preheat the oven to 350° F.

Oil a baking pan (including sides of pan).

In a mixing bowl or food processor, blend the mascarpone cheese with the chives, parsley, garlic and shallot. Season to taste with salt and pepper. Lay the fillets out on a clean surface. Using a spatula, spread the cheese mixture evenly over each fillet. Roll each fillet into a bundle and place the rolls, seam-side down in the oiled baking pan. Season the outside of the rolls with salt and pepper and then sprinkle them with the lemon juice. Pour the wine and water into the bottom of the pan. Bake the fish for about 10-15 minutes, or until it is just cooked through.

Transfer the fish rolls to a plate and set aside to keep warm. Transfer the pan juices to a small saucepan and bring to a boil over high heat. Stir in the sugar. Lower heat to a simmer and cook for about 10 minutes, or until slightly reduced. Add the butter, piece by piece, stirring until just barely melted.

To serve: Place a fish packet in the center of each serving plate and drizzle with the sauce. Garnish with lemon wedges and fresh herbs.

CHEF'S TIP

The most common varieties of "sole" sold in the Northwest are petrale sole and English (Dover) sole. Other white fish, including flounder and halibut, are all interchangeable in recipes that call for sole.

Hook & Line Lingcod, Steamed Clams & Mussels

HOOK & LINE LINGCOD
STEAMED CLAMS & MUSSELS

GARLIC MASHED POTATOES

4 garlic cloves

Olive oil

3 large russet potatoes, peeled and diced

Water to cover

1/2 tablespoon salt

1/4 cup (1/2 stick) butter

Milk or half-and-half as needed

Salt and freshly ground black pepper to taste

ZUCCHINI WRAPS

1 or 2 large zucchini, rinsed, ends trimmed

1 tablespoon olive oil

Salt and freshly ground black pepper to taste

FRESH, HOOK-AND-LINE-CAUGHT LINGCOD IS A FAVORITE ON THE OREGON COAST. SWEET AND DELICATE, IT IS BEST WHEN SIMPLY PREPARED. IN THIS DISH, A SIGNATURE ITEM AT THE STEPHANIE INN, THE FISH RESTS ON A BED OF GARLIC-MASHED POTATOES SURROUNDED BY A THIN WRAP OF SAUTÉED ZUCCHINI. MUSSELS AND CLAMS STEAMED IN WHITE WINE, HERBS, AND GARLIC SURROUND THE FISH. YOU CAN SUBSTITUTE ANY FRESH, DELICATELY-FLAVORED WHITE FISH, SUCH AS SOLE OR HALIBUT. TO PREPARE A SIMPLER VERSION AT HOME, YOU CAN SKIP THE ZUCCHINI WRAP AND SIMPLY SET THE FISH ON A BED OF MASHED POTATOES SURROUNDED BY FRESHLY STEAMED CLAMS AND MUSSELS. POUR A BUTTERY CHARDONNAY OR PINOT GRIS TO SERVE WITH THIS DELICATE DISH.

To prepare the Garlic Mashed Potatoes: Preheat the oven to 350° F. Place the garlic cloves in a pan and sprinkle with a little olive oil. Roast the garlic until it is tender, about 15 minutes. Place the diced potatoes in a medium saucepan, add water to cover, and a pinch of salt. Bring the water to a boil over high heat, then reduce the heat to a simmer and cook until the potatoes are tender when pierced with a fork. Drain the cooking water. Add the roasted garlic and butter. Mash, using a potato masher. Add enough milk or half-and-half to give the right consistency (semi-firm and smooth). Season the potatoes to taste with salt and pepper. Cover and set aside to keep warm.

To prepare the Zucchini Wraps: Slice the zucchini lengthwise into 1/4-inch slices. Season the slices with salt and pepper. Heat the olive oil in a large skillet and sauté the slices on each side until just pliable, about 1 to 2 minutes. Remove from the heat to a plate and set aside.

To prepare the Lingcod Fillets: Increase the oven heat to 350° F. Heat the canola oil in a skillet over medium-high heat. Season the lingcod fillets with salt and pepper and lay them gently into the hot oil. Sear the fish about 3 minutes on the presentation side (best-looking side), until golden. Place the fillets seared-side-up in the preheated oven until cooked through, about 3 to 5 minutes, depending on thickness.

To prepare the Garlic-Steamed Clams and Mussels: Heat the olive oil in a large stockpot over medium-high heat. Stir in the shallots, minced garlic, saffron and diced tomatoes. Cook for about 3 minutes, or until the tomatoes are soft. Add the clams and mussels, then pour the white wine over the shellfish. Cover and steam until the clams and mussels have opened, about 7 to 10 minutes.

To assemble and serve: Using a large ice cream scoop, place a mound of mashed potatoes in the center of each serving plate. Wrap the sides of each potato mound with strips of zucchini (see photo below and on next page). Place a lingcod fillet on top of the potatoes and garnish with a sprig of parsley. Remove the top shell from the clams and mussels and arrange the shellfish around the cod. Drizzle the clams and mussels with their cooking broth.

LINGCOD FILLETS

2 tablespoons Canola oil

4 6-ounce lingcod fillets, deboned

Salt and freshly ground black pepper to taste

GARLIC-STEAMED CLAMS & MUSSELS

2 tablespoons olive oil

1 shallot, minced

3 garlic cloves, minced

Pinch of saffron (optional)

2 medium tomatoes, finely diced

1½ dozen Manila clams in the shell, scrubbed clean

1½ dozen mussels in the shell, scrubbed clean and debearded, if necessary

2 cups dry white wine

4 sprigs Italian parsley for garnish

SERVES 4

ROASTED PORTOBELLO MUSHROOMS

1   cup olive oil

1/2   cup balsamic vinegar

1/2   cup water

4   portobello mushrooms, cleaned and stems removed

Kosher salt and freshly ground black pepper to taste

LEMONGRASS ESSENCE

2   cups heavy cream

1/4   cup dry white wine

1   stalk lemongrass, sliced into 2-inch pieces

2   garlic cloves, minced

Juice of 1/2 lemon

NORTHWEST SALMON
ROASTED PORTOBELLO MUSHROOMS & LEMONGRASS ESSENCE

FRESH SALMON FROM COLD PACIFIC WATERS IS LINE-CAUGHT AND DELIVERED FRESH TO THE STEPHANIE INN KITCHEN BY LOCAL FISHERMEN JUST HOURS AFTER IT IS CAUGHT. IT DOESN'T GET ANY BETTER. IN THIS RECIPE, THE SALMON IS SERVED WITH ROASTED PORTOBELLO MUSHROOMS FILLED WITH SHREDDED NAPA CABBAGE, AND TOPPED WITH AN ELEGANT CREAM SAUCE FLAVORED WITH LEMONGRASS AND WHITE WINE. AT THE INN, THIS IS SERVED WITH A BED OF CREAMY MASHED POTATOES ON ONE SIDE AND A CLUSTER OF CRISPY FRIED POTATOES ON THE OTHER. POUR AN EARTHY PINOT NOIR OR RED BURGUNDY TO HIGHLIGHT THE RICH, EARTHY FLAVORS OF THE MUSHROOMS AND SALMON.

Preheat the oven to 375° F.

Grease a baking pan.

To prepare the Roasted Portobello Mushrooms: Using a teaspoon, gently scrape out the dark gills from each mushroom cap. Discard the gills. Whisk together the olive oil, balsamic vinegar and water in a large bowl. Add the mushrooms and toss with the vinaigrette. Set the mushrooms on a greased baking pan and roast for about 20 minutes, or until soft. Reserve and keep warm.

To make the Lemongrass Essence: Combine the cream, wine, lemongrass, garlic and lemon juice in a saucepan over medium-high heat. Simmer until the mixture is reduced by one-half, about 12 to 15 minutes. Transfer the sauce to a blender or food processor and purée. Strain the sauce and return it to the saucepan to keep warm over low heat.

To prepare the Salmon Fillets: Sprinkle the salmon fillets with salt and pepper and set aside. Heat 2 tablespoons of olive oil in a skillet over medium-high heat. Sear the fillets on one side, until golden (about 3 minutes). Transfer to a baking pan, seared side up, and place in the oven for about 5 to 7 minutes, or until the salmon is just cooked through and flakes easily with a fork.

To prepare the Napa Cabbage: Melt the butter in a skillet over medium heat. Add the cabbage and stir well to coat with the butter. Stir in the water and simmer over medium heat until the cabbage is soft and translucent, about 5 minutes. Drain the cabbage and season to taste with salt and pepper.

To assemble and serve: Place a roasted mushroom cap, gills facing up, on each of four plates. Spoon a portion of the cooked cabbage inside each mushroom. Place a salmon fillet next to the mushroom on each plate. Drizzle the salmon and mushrooms with the lemongrass sauce.

SALMON FILLETS

4   6-ounce salmon fillets, deboned

2   tablespoons olive oil

Kosher salt and freshly ground black pepper to taste

NAPA CABBAGE

1   tablespoon butter or canola oil

3   cups julienned Napa cabbage

Water to cover

Salt and freshly ground black pepper to taste

SERVES 4

Pacific Northwest Salmon

Revered throughout history as one of the tastiest, most magnificent foods, wild Pacific salmon is elemental in defining Pacific Northwest cuisine. Early in the 19th century, explorers Lewis and Clark described rivers thick with salmon, noting that Native fishermen often caught up to twenty huge salmon an hour.

As spring approaches each year, rivers rise swiftly with rainwater and snowmelt, rousing young salmon from their gravel nests under the river floor. Soon these tiny fish will fight their way downriver to the ocean, where they will feed and grow into adults. Depending on their species, salmon may live in the sea up to five years.

Eventually succumbing to their instinctual homing devices, salmon begin battling their way home to their birth-streams, fighting thousands of miles of powerful ocean currents, dams, waterfalls, rapids, hungry bears, and more.

When the salmon first enter the rivers, they are fat from months of ocean feeding. Once they leave the ocean, they stop eating, depleting their own stores of fat for nourishment. Their sole purpose, once they arrive "home," is to produce eggs or spawn, creating new life before they die.

The unique phenomenon of salmon finding their way home to their natal streams or rivers, after spending years at sea, and traveling thousands of miles through unfamiliar waters, is still a great mystery. Some attribute it to the salmon's sense of salinity in the water. Others suspect electric currents and magnetism, the pull of the sun and the moon, or imprint and recall within the salmon's psyche.

Salmon was highly regarded by Northwest Natives as their primary food source. According to ancient tradition, spring salmon must be cooked under an open sky where it is touched by the wind, the air, and the sun. Slow-burning Northwest alder is the favored wood for cooking. The fire burns down to glowing embers that emit slow, steady heat for cooking.

WILD SALMON OCEAN SPECIES OF THE PACIFIC NORTHWEST

KING, CHINOOK, TYEE, or BLACKMOUTH (Oncorhynchus tshawytscha): This is the largest and rarest of the Pacific species, averaging 15 to 40 pounds, with some specimens weighing up to 100 pounds. Kings, whose flesh color ranges from a rich "salmon" shade to almost white, are highly prized for their fat content, which imparts complex flavor and rich texture. Kings are mainly available from May to September. The fattest King salmon are considered the "king of kings." Topping the list are Columbia River Chinooks, Alaskan Yukon Kings and Copper River Kings.

COHO, SILVER (O. kisutch): Average market size for the Coho salmon is 5 to 10 pounds, although some can grow to over 20 pounds. Like the meat of King salmon, Coho meat, which ranges in color from rich orange-red to pale pink, forms large flakes when cooked. Cohos are firm-fleshed and extremely flavorful. Their season runs from July through September.

SOCKEYE, REDS, or BLUEBACKS (O. nerka): The deep red flesh of Sockeye is tightly grained, with a robust flavor. These are the second fattest of the Pacific salmon, generally weighing 5 to 7 pounds. They are available from late May through July.

CHUM, KETA, DOG, or FALL SALMON (O. keta): Chum meat is less fatty than other salmon, and usually paler in color, although many chums have a good reddish-orange color and unique earthy flavor. These fish are available from July through October.

PINK, HUMPIE (O. gorbuscha): Pinks are the smallest and most abundant of the Pacific salmon. The meat, as the name suggests, is usually pink in color and delicately flavored. Because of their small size, Pinks are excellent for grilling whole. Most of the Pink harvest is canned.

PLANKED SALMON

Planking is an ancient method of cooking fish that is credited to the Swedes, who were doing it more than a thousand years ago. In America, planking reached its vogue during the Gay Nineties in Chicago, when the popular Fair Store on State Street stocked stacks of planks priced from 15 cents up, according to size.

Over the years, different woods, such as oak and alder, have been used for planking fish, but Western Red Cedar, which is native to the Pacific Northwest, is especially favored. This highly aromatic wood imparts an incomparably complex flavor with spicy and woodsy tones that complement salmon.

Traditionally, planks are never washed, but rather scraped clean down to the grain after each use, and then rubbed shiny with vegetable oil, preferably olive oil. Prior to cooking, the plank is preheated in the oven and brushed again with vegetable oil. Planked fish is often bordered with mashed potatoes and steamed vegetables just before serving. The plank is then returned to the oven and broiled until the potatoes are golden brown.

CEDAR-PLANK-BAKED SALMON
DIJON BEURRE BLANC

BAKING FISH ON A CEDAR PLANK INFUSES IT WITH A RUSTIC SMOKINESS THAT IS REMINISCENT OF NATIVE AMERICAN SALMON ROASTED OVER A CEDAR FIRE. YOU CAN FIND CEDAR PLANKS FOR THIS PURPOSE IN MOST KITCHEN SHOPS. SERVE THE SALMON WITH COUSCOUS, RICE, OR MASHED POTATOES AND FRESH SAUTÉED VEGETABLES. A NORTHWEST PINOT NOIR OR RED BURGUNDY WILL HIGHLIGHT THE DELICIOUS SMOKY FLAVORS IN THIS DISH.

Preheat the oven to 350° F.

To prepare the salmon: Rub a seasoned cedar baking plank (See the Chef's Tip below) with olive oil and place in the oven for 10 to 15 minutes. Meanwhile, rub the salmon with olive oil and sprinkle with Kosher salt and freshly ground black pepper. Heat about 1 tablespoon of olive oil in a skillet or grill over medium-high heat. When the skillet is hot, add the salmon, presentation-side down and sear for about 2 minutes. (This will add color and help seal in flavorful juices.) Place the salmon on the hot plank (seared side up), and bake until it is just cooked through, about 15 to 20 minutes. (The meat should still be moist, but should flake easily with a fork.)

To prepare the Dijon Beurre Blanc: While the salmon bakes, cut the chilled butter into small cubes and set on a plate in the freezer to chill further. Place the shallots in a medium saucepan, together with the white wine and vinegar. Bring the mixture to a boil and reduce until just 1 tablespoon of liquid is left. Add the cream and simmer 1 more minute. Reduce the heat to low and whisk in the cold butter, one piece at a time, whisking well after each addition. Whisk in the lemon juice, chopped parsley, and Dijon mustard. Season to taste with salt and white pepper. To keep the sauce warm, set the saucepan in a pan of warm water, or place in a Thermos-type container until served.

To serve: Arrange the salmon fillets on four serving plates. Ladle the Dijon Beurre Blanc around the sides of each fillet and lightly over the top.

CHEF'S TIP

To season a new cedar plank, rinse it in warm water and place it in a slow oven (300° F) to dry. Rub the warm plank liberally with olive oil or canola oil and set it back in the oven for 10 minutes.

SALMON FILLETS

4   6- to 8-ounce salmon steaks or fillets, deboned

2 to 3 tablespoons olive oil

Kosher salt and freshly ground black pepper to taste

Seasoned cedar plank

DIJON BEURRE BLANC

1½   cups (3 sticks) butter, chilled

2   shallots, peeled and minced

1   cup dry white wine

1   tablespoon white wine vinegar

Juice of 1/2 lemon

2   tablespoons heavy cream

2   tablespoons finely chopped fresh parsley

1   tablespoon prepared Dijon mustard

Salt and white pepper to taste

SERVES 4

Chardonnay-Poached Salmon

2　cups Chardonnay or
　　Pinot Gris wine

1　cup cold water

1/2　medium onion, diced

1　large carrot, diced

2　stalks celery, diced

4　sprigs fresh thyme

2　bay leaves

4　6- to 8-ounce salmon fillets,
　　skinned and deboned

Salt and freshly ground black pepper
　　to taste

1/4　cup butter (1/2 stick), chilled
　　and diced

Chopped fresh parsley for garnish

2　cups wilted spinach

Garlic-Sauteéd Mushrooms
　　(see Recipe Index;
　　use 1/2 recipe)

In this dish, the flavorful cooking juices from the salmon are reduced and whisked with butter to create a delicious, creamy sauce. Serve with wilted spinach, sautéed mushrooms, and Pinot Gris or a rich, buttery Chardonnay.

In a large skillet, combine the wine, water, onion, carrot, celery, thyme, and bay leaves. Bring the mixture to a boil over high heat. Reduce the heat to medium low and simmer for about 10 minutes.

Meanwhile, season the salmon fillets on both sides with salt and pepper. Place the fillets in the hot poaching liquid. Cover, and cook until just tender, about 10 to 12 minutes. (The salmon should flake easily with a fork, and should be cooked just through.)

Remove the salmon from the poaching liquid to a platter with a slotted spoon and cover to keep warm. Strain 6 ounces (3/4 cup) of the poaching liquid through a sieve into a small saucepan and bring it to a boil over medium-high heat. Reduce the heat to a rapid simmer, and cook, about 12 minutes, or until the liquid is reduced by half. Turn the heat to low and whisk in the chilled butter, 1 tablespoon at a time, until the butter is incorporated. Cover to keep warm.

To serve: Place a salmon fillet in the center of each of four pre-warmed plates. Ladle the sauce over the salmon and sprinkle with chopped parsley. Arrange wilted spinach and sautéed mushrooms on each plate.

Serves 4

Coconut Curried Prawns

SERVE THESE PRAWNS OVER STEAMED JASMINE OR BASMATI RICE AND GARNISH WITH TOASTED COCONUT AND CHOPPED CILANTRO. POUR A CHILLED DRY RIESLING OR GEWÜRZTRAMINER TO HIGHLIGHT THE SPICY, SWEET FLAVORS OF THE CURRIED PRAWNS. THOSE WHO ARE WARY OF SPICY-HOT DISHES MIGHT WANT TO CAREFULLY TASTE THE RED CURRY SAUCE BEFORE ADDING THE FULL TEASPOON OF IT TO THE RECIPE.

24	medium prawns (about 2-inches long), shelled, tailed, and deveined
1	tablespoon butter
1	tablespoon vegetable oil
2	garlic cloves, minced
2	shallots, minced
1/4	cup chopped chives
1/4	cup chopped fresh cilantro
1/4	cup dry white wine
	Juice of 1/2 lime
	Juice of 1/2 lemon
1/2	cup (8 oz) unsweetened coconut milk
1/2	cup vegetable broth, preferably homemade (scc Recipe Index)
1	teaspoon red curry paste
	Salt and freshly ground black pepper to taste
1/2	cup toasted coconut for garnish
1/4	cup chopped chives

Melt the butter and oil in a large saucepan over medium-high heat. Stir in the garlic, shallots, chives, and cilantro, and cook for about 2 minutes, or until the garlic is tender. Add the prawns and cook until they start to turn orange. Add the wine and continue cooking until the prawns are bright orange and cooked through. Stir in the lime and lemon juice. Simmer the sauce rapidly, for about 10 minutes, or until it is slightly reduced. Add the coconut milk, chicken broth ,and curry paste, and continue to cook to reduce, stirring often, for about 15 minutes, or until the sauce has thickened slightly.

Remove the prawns from the sauce with a slotted spoon and cover to keep warm. Bring the sauce to a rapid simmer and reduce it until it is thick and has a creamy consistency, about 3 minutes. Season the sauce to taste with salt and pepper. Stir in the cooked prawns and heat until the prawns are warmed through.

To serve: Spoon the prawns over steamed rice and garnish with toasted coconut and chopped chives.

SERVES 4

Prawn Risotto
Garlic & Wine-Simmered Prawns

The chefs at The Stephanie Inn often serve this dish as an appetizer. However, when served with Grilled Asparagus (see Recipe Index), and a loaf of freshly baked bread, this is a delicious light and healthful meal. A glass of chilled white wine makes a fine companion.

Prawn Risotto

4	large prawns, shelled, deveined, and diced
2	tablespoons olive oil
2	shallots, minced
2	garlic cloves, minced
1	cup Arborio rice
1	cup dry white wine
2	cups water, as needed
1	tablespoon chopped fresh parsley

Juice of 1/2 lemon

1/2	cup freshly grated Parmesan cheese

Salt and freshly ground black pepper to taste

Garlic & Wine-Simmered Prawns

20	large prawns, shelled and deveined (tails intact)
2	tablespoons olive oil
1	tablespoon butter
2	shallots, minced
3	garlic cloves, minced
1	tablespoon chopped fresh parsley
1	tablespoon minced chives
2	tablespoons fresh lemon juice
1/2	cup white wine

To prepare the Prawn Risotto: Heat the olive oil in a large saucepan over medium-high heat. Add the prawns, shallots and garlic, and cook, stirring often, just until golden. Stir in the rice, then stir continuously until the rice begins to brown. Pour in a little bit of the wine, mixing well, until the wine is absorbed by the rice. Stir in the next bit of wine, and repeat the process. Next, add water, a bit at a time, (adding more water as necessary), until the rice is cooked al dente (cooked through, but firm to the tooth). Stir in the chopped parsley, lemon juice, and grated cheese. Season to taste with salt and pepper.

To prepare the Garlic & Wine-Simmered Prawns: Heat the olive oil and butter in a large skillet over medium-high heat. Add the shallots and garlic and sauté, stirring often, for about 2 minutes, or until golden. Add the prawns, lemon juice, and white wine. Cook, stirring often, until the prawns are bright orange and cooked through, about 5 to 7 minutes.

To assemble and serve: Scoop a mound of risotto onto each serving plate (about 1/2-cup per serving, as an appetizer) and surround with the poached prawns. Drizzle the poaching sauce from the prawns over the prawns and risotto.

Serves 4 as an appetizer or
2 as a main dish

GARLICKY SEAFOOD STEW

12 ounces salmon fillet, skinned, deboned, and cut into 1/2-inch pieces

12 ounces halibut fillet, skinned, deboned, and cut into 1/2-inch pieces

16 medium prawns, shelled and deveined

2 medium Yukon Gold or red potatoes, diced and cooked in salted water until tender

3 tablespoons olive or canola oil

3 garlic cloves, minced

1 large onion, diced

1 leek (white part only), finely sliced

2 large tomatoes, diced

1/2 cup dry white wine

1½ cups fish stock (see Recipe Index)

1½ cups heavy cream

Salt and freshly ground black pepper to taste

Juice of 1/2 lemon

Chopped chives or green onions for garnish

SERVES 4

BRIMMING WITH FRESH SEAFOOD, INCLUDING SALMON, HALIBUT, AND PRAWNS, THIS FLAVORFUL SEAFOOD STEW MAKES A DELICIOUS ONE-DISH MEAL. SERVE WITH HOT, CRUSTY BREAD ON THE SIDE AND POUR A FULL-BODIED PINOT GRIS OR CHARDONNAY FOR A FINISHING TOUCH.

Heat the olive oil in a stockpot over medium heat. Stir in the garlic, onion and leeks. Cover the pot and cook until the vegetables are tender, stirring often. Stir in the diced tomatoes and cook for about 12 minutes or until the tomatoes are softened. Add the wine and fish stock. Increase the heat to a boil over high heat and then reduce the heat to a rapid simmer and cook for about 12 minutes, or until the stock has thickened slightly.

Add the seafood and cook for about 10 to 12 minutes, (stirring very gently and turning occasionally), until the seafood is just cooked through. Reduce the heat to a simmer; pour in the heavy cream, and season to taste with salt, pepper, and lemon juice.

To serve: Dish into pre-warmed soup bowls and garnish with chopped chives or green onions.

NORTH COAST STEAMED CLAMS

IN THE PACIFIC NORTHWEST, STEPHANIE INN CHEFS HAVE ACCESS TO A NUMBER OF FLAVORFUL LOCAL BEERS, INCLUDING SOME BREWED IN THE TOWN OF CANNON BEACH. OF COURSE, YOU CAN USE YOUR FAVORITE LOCAL BEER OR ALE IN THIS DISH. HOT, CRUSTY BREAD AND A COLD BEER NICELY ROUND OUT THIS DISH.

Rinse the clams under cold running water, *discarding any that are opened and don't stay closed when the shells are pinched together.* Set the rinsed clams aside.

In a large saucepan, heat the olive oil over medium-high heat. Stir in the tomatoes, garlic, green onion, red onion, and lime juice. Cook until the tomatoes are softened. Stir in the clams and pour the beer over the mixture. Cover and bring to a boil until the clams open, about 8 to 10 minutes. Transfer to a serving bowl. Season to taste with salt and pepper and hot red chili flakes. Garnish with sliced green onions.

2	pounds Manila clams or other small steamer clams
3	tablespoons olive oil
4	large tomatoes, cored anddiced
3	garlic cloves, minced
3	green onions, rinsed and diced
1/2	red onion, diced
	Juice of 1 lime
6	ounces (3/4 cup) beer or ale
	Salt and freshly ground black pepper to taste
	Hot red chili flakes to taste
1/4	cup sliced green onions

CHEF'S TIP

It is best to buy and use live clams the same day. If you need to store them overnight, place the clams in the refrigerator in a bowl and cover with a damp cloth.

SERVES 2 AS A MAIN DISH
OR 4 AS AN APPETIZER

DUNGENESS CRAB CAKES
LEMON AIOLI

SERVED WITH A GARLICKY LEMON AIOLI AND A GLASS OF CHILLED SAUVIGNON BLANC OR SEMILLON, THESE CRAB CAKES ARE THE ULTIMATE. UNLIKE MANY CRAB CAKES THAT ARE FILLED WITH BREADCRUMBS OR OTHER FILLERS, THESE ARE PURE CRAB, BOUND LIGHTLY WITH A FISH MOUSSELINE. AT THE INN, THE CHEFS TOP THE CRAB CAKES WITH A THIN SLICE OF LEMON AND DRIZZLE A TOUCH OF BALSAMIC SYRUP AROUND THE EDGES. THE DISH IS GARNISHED WITH FRESH CHOPPED CHIVES, AND, IN SEASON, FIDDLEHEAD FERNS.

CRAB CAKES

1/2	pound cooked Dungeness crabmeat
2	ounces shelled, tailed, and de-veined prawn or shrimp meat
2	ounces fresh scallops
4	tablespoons heavy cream

Juice of 1/2 lemon

1/4	cup chopped chives
1/4	cup chopped fresh parsley

Salt and freshly ground black pepper to taste

LEMON AIOLI

Makes about 3/4 cup

2	egg yolks

Juice of 1/2 lemon

1	garlic clove, minced
1	teaspoon Dijon mustard
1/2	cup olive oil

Water if needed

BALSAMIC SYRUP

1	cup balsamic vinegar

Salt and freshly ground black pepper to taste

Fresh chopped chives for garnish

SERVES 2 AS A MAIN COURSE OR 4 AS AN APPETIZER

To prepare the Crab Cake mixture: Pick through the cooked crabmeat and remove shells. Set the crabmeat aside. In a food processor, combine the prawns, scallops, cream, lemon juice, and salt and pepper to taste. Purée the mixture until smooth. Transfer the mousseline to a mixing bowl and gently fold in the crabmeat, chives, and parsley. Cover the mixture with plastic wrap and chill until needed.

To make the Lemon Aioli: In a mixing bowl, whisk the egg yolks until thick and lemon colored. Whisk in the lemon juice, garlic, and mustard, mixing well. Gradually add the olive oil, mixing steadily, until it is incorporated. If the mixture is too thick, substitute a bit of water for the oil. Season to taste with salt and pepper. Cover and store in the refrigerator until needed.

To make the Balsamic Syrup: Pour 1 cup Balsamic vinegar into a saucepan, bring to a boil, and simmer rapidly, until it is reduced to the consistency of maple syrup.

To complete the Crab Cakes: Heat 2 tablespoons of olive oil or butter in a large skillet over medium-high heat. Form 1/4-cup portions of the crab cake mixture into small patties, about 1/2-inch thick. Fry the cakes on both sides until golden brown, about 4 minutes per side.

To serve: Arrange hot crab cakes on a plate and sprinkle with chopped chives. Drizzle a touch of Balsamic Syrup around the edges and serve with Lemon Aioli on the side.

CHEF'S TIP

The crab cake mixture can be prepared up to 8 hours in advance. The Lemon Aioli will keep, covered, up to three days in the refrigerator.

Seared Halibut Fillets
Pesto Cream Sauce

Seared Halibut Fillets

4   6-ounce halibut fillets (1-inch thick), skinned and deboned

Kosher salt and freshly ground black pepper to taste

3   tablespoons olive oil

2   cups dry white wine

Water, as needed

Juice of 2 lemons

Pesto Cream Sauce

1   cup heavy cream

1/4 cup dry white wine

1/3 cup fish (see Recipe Index) or chicken stock

1   shallot, minced

1   garlic clove, minced

Juice of 1/2 lemon

1   tablespoon basil pesto (See Recipe Index)

Salt and freshly ground black pepper to taste

Fresh or fried basil leaves for garnish

Serves 4

Halibut season is always a cause for celebration in the Pacific Northwest. With its snowy-white flesh, meaty texture, and sea-fresh flavor, it is especially good topped with a creamy sauce flavored with basil pesto. Chefs at The Stephanie Inn often top this dish with basil leaves that have been fried in hot oil until crisp. This dish calls for a buttery Chardonnay loaded with tropical fruit flavors. The Pesto Cream Sauce can be prepared ahead and reheated before serving.

To prepare the Seared Halibut Fillets: Preheat the oven to 350° F. Season the fillets liberally with salt and pepper. Heat the olive oil in a large skillet over medium-high heat. Place the fillets in the hot oil and sear on one side until golden, about 3 minutes. Oil a rectangular baking pan (approximately 9-inches by 11-inches, with sides), and place the halibut, seared side up in the pan. Pour in the wine and water (as needed) to cover the bottom of the pan with at least 1-inch of liquid. Pour the lemon juice over the fish and bake for about 15 to 20 minutes, or until the fish is firm to the touch and no longer opaque.

To make the Pesto Cream Sauce: In a saucepan, whisk together the cream, wine, fish stock, shallots, garlic, and lemon juice. Bring the mixture to a boil over medium-high heat. Reduce the heat to a rapid simmer and cook, stirring occasionally, for about 15 minutes or until the sauce is reduced to a creamy consistency. Strain the sauce through a sieve into a clean saucepan and whisk in the pesto. Season the sauce to taste with lemon, salt and pepper, and reheat just before serving.

To serve: Place the halibut fillets in the center of each pre-warmed plate. Ladle 2 to 4 tablespoons of the pesto sauce around the halibut and drizzle a little more sauce over the top of each fillet. Garnish with fresh or fried basil leaves.

Sautéed Oysters
Prosciutto & Browned Garlic Butter

Specializing in innovative Northwest fare, chefs at The Stephanie Inn gain inspiration from fresh local Willapa Bay oysters. Here, they are topped with a golden brown butter sauce and sliced prosciutto. Recommended wines include Champagne or sparkling wine, Chardonnay, Pinot Blanc, and Pinot Gris.

In a shallow dish, combine the flour, cornmeal, salt, and pepper. Dredge oysters lightly in the mixture, shaking off excess flour. Heat oil in a skillet over medium-high heat. Gently add the oysters and sauté on both sides until golden brown, about 5 minutes per side. Remove the oysters from the oil with a slotted spoon and drain on paper towels. Keep warm.

Discard the cooking oil and wipe the skillet clean with paper towels. Place the skillet over medium-high heat, add the butter, and cook until the butter sizzles and turns golden brown. Reduce the heat to low and stir in the minced garlic and lemon juice. Cook for about 3 minutes.

To serve: Place 12 oysters on each pre-warmed serving plate. Drizzle with the browned butter and distribute the prosciutto slices evenly over the oysters. Top each oyster with a sprinkling of chopped chives. Serve hot.

24	small or medium oysters, shucked and drained
2	tablespoons all-purpose flour
2	tablespoons yellow cornmeal
1/2	teaspoon salt
1/4	teaspoon freshly ground black pepper
2	tablespoons vegetable oil
3	tablespoons butter
1	garlic clove, minced
1	tablespoon fresh lemon juice
2	ounces prosciutto, sliced into paper-thin slices
1	tablespoon finely chopped chives for garnish

Serves 2

SAUTÉED OYSTERS
GREEN ONION AIOLI

SEASONED WITH FRESH GREEN ONIONS (SCALLIONS), THIS GARLICKY AIOLI ADDS A FRESH BITE OF HEAT TO SWEET, NORTH COAST OYSTERS. SERVE WITH A CRISP GREEN SALAD AND CRUSTY BREAD. CHAMPAGNE, SPARKLING WINE, OR A ZESTY PINOT GRIS IS A DELICIOUS MATCH WITH THESE CRISPY OYSTERS.

GREEN ONION AIOLI

Makes about 1 1/2 cups

2   large egg yolks

Juice of 1/2 lemon

1   cup extra virgin olive oil

1   garlic clove, minced

1/2 bunch green onions, finely chopped

Salt and white pepper to taste

SAUTÉED OYSTERS

32   medium oysters, shucked and drained

1/2 cup cornmeal

1/2 cup all-purpose flour

Salt and freshly ground black pepper to taste

2   tablespoons fresh lemon juice

4   tablespoons canola oil for cooking, or as needed

To make the Green Onion Aioli: In the bowl of a food processor, process the egg yolks until pale and thick. Gradually add the lemon juice, then the garlic. Slowly add the olive oil, scraping down the sides as necessary. Transfer the mixture to a mixing bowl. Stir in the chopped green onions. Season to taste with salt and white pepper. Aioli may be stored, covered, in the refrigerator up to 5 days.

To prepare the Sautéed Oysters: Drain the oysters on paper towels. Combine the cornmeal and flour in a shallow pan. Season the oysters with salt and pepper, and the 2 tablespoons lemon juice. Lightly dredge the oysters in the cornmeal mixture, shaking off any excess. Set them aside on a clean plate. Heat 2 tablespoons of canola oil in a skillet over medium-high heat. When the oil is sizzling, quickly place the oysters in the pan, cooking in batches if necessary, so you don't overcrowd the pan. Cook the oysters about 2 to 3 minutes on each side, until golden brown. Add more oil, if necessary, and heat it thoroughly. If cooking in batches, before adding more oysters, use a slotted spoon to remove any burnt pieces of cornmeal. Keep warm in a 200° F oven until ready to serve with the Green Onion Aioli.

SERVES 4

Dijon Marinade

1	tablespoon Dijon mustard
1	cup dry red wine
1/2	cup olive oil
1	bunch fresh parsley, stemmed and finely chopped
1	bunch fresh thyme, stemmed and finely chopped
4	garlic cloves, minced
4	tablespoons dark soy sauce (or 3 tablespoons regular soy sauce and 1 tablespoon molasses)
2	domestic, or 3 New Zealand racks of lamb (approximately 1/2 pound, or 3 to 6 lamb chops per person)

Salt and freshly ground black pepper to taste

Canola oil, as needed

Dried Cherry Port Sauce

Reserved pan drippings from the lamb plus enough veal or vegetable stock to equal 1/4 cup (see Recipe Index)

1	cup port wine
2	cups dried cherries
4	tablespoons (1/2 stick) butter, chilled

Salt and freshly ground black pepper to taste

Fresh mint leaves for garnish

Spring Lamb Chops
Dried Cherry Port Sauce

RAISED IN THE GOLDEN FIELDS OF EASTERN WASHINGTON AND OREGON, NORTHWEST LAMB IS MILD AND SUCCULENT. THE RACKS OF LOCAL LAMB ARE A BIT LARGER THAN THOSE FROM NEW ZEALAND, WHICH WOULD MAKE A FINE SUBSTITUTE. PLAN ON 2 WHOLE RACKS OF NORTHWEST LAMB, OR 3 RACKS OF NEW ZEALAND LAMB TO FEED SIX PEOPLE (ABOUT 3 TO 6 CHOPS PER PERSON). PLAN TO MARINATE THE LAMB FOR AT LEAST 2 HOURS, OR OVERNIGHT. SERVED WITH GOAT CHEESE-STUFFED POTATOES (SEE RECIPE INDEX) AND SAUTÉED SPINACH, THIS DISH IS FIT FOR ANY SPECIAL OCCASION. CHOOSE A RICH, VELVETY MERLOT OR CABERNET SAUVIGNON TO COMPLEMENT THE EARTHINESS OF THE LAMB AND BRING OUT THE CHERRY FLAVOR IN THE SAUCE.

To make the Dijon Marinade: Whisk together all marinade ingredients in a large, shallow pan or mixing bowl. Add the lamb, turning to coat all sides. Cover and place it in the refrigerator for 2 hours or overnight.

Remove the lamb from the marinade and set it on paper towels to drain. Season the lamb racks lightly with kosher salt and pepper. Heat the canola oil in a large skillet over medium-high heat and sear the lamb racks on each side, until they are golden brown (working in batches, if necessary.)

Preheat the oven to 350° F. Place the lamb on an oiled baking pan and roast until a meat thermometer inserted in the center reads 115° F (for tender, mouth-watering rare lamb) or until it is cooked to your preference. Pour off the pan juices and reserve them for the sauce. Cover the lamb to keep it warm.

To make the Dried Cherry Port Sauce: Place the reserved pan juices in a saucepan and bring to a boil over high heat. Stir in the port and dried cherries and continue to simmer rapidly until reduced by one-half, about 12 minutes. Remove the sauce from the heat and whisk in the chilled butter, one tablespoon at a time. Season the sauce to taste with salt and pepper. Cover to keep warm until ready to serve.

To serve: Slice the lamb racks into individual chops and fan out on serving plates. Ladle Dried Cherry Port Sauce around the lamb and drizzle some over the top of the chops (approximately 2 tablespoons per serving). Garnish with fresh mint leaves.

SERVES 6

Seared Pork Loin, Savoy Cabbage, Apple & Creamy Polenta

SEARED PORK LOIN
SAVOY CABBAGE, APPLE & CREAMY POLENTA

24   ounces pork tenderloin

Salt and freshly ground black pepper
    to taste

3   tablespoons olive oil

4   whole leaves of Savoy cabbage
    or Swiss chard with stems
    attached

Salted water to cover

3   tablespoons butter

3   tablespoons sugar

2   tart apples, peeled and sliced
    (or formed into balls using a
    melon-baller)

2   cups prepared Creamy Polenta
    (see Recipe Index)

SLICES OF PORK TENDERLOIN ARE CAPPED WITH A FLAVORFUL SAUCE AND SERVED WITH CREAMY POLENTA TOPPED WITH CRISPY FRIED ONIONS. THE STEPHANIE INN CHEFS USE A MELON BALLER TO SCOOP THE APPLES INTO SMALL ROUNDS, BUT YOU CAN ALSO SLICE THE APPLES INTO THIN SLICES. FOR A SPECIAL GARNISH, BACON IS SLICED INTO THIN STRIPS AND FRIED UNTIL IT IS SLIGHTLY CRISP, THEN WRAPPED AROUND THE HANDLE OF A WOODEN SPOON WHILE STILL HOT TO CREATE A CURLICUE. THIS DISH CALLS FOR A LUSH, FRUITY, RED WINE, SUCH AS A MERLOT, ZINFANDEL OR SYRAH AS ITS ACCOMPANIMENT.

To prepare the Seared Pork Loin: Preheat the oven to 350° F. Trim any excess fat from the tenderloin and season all sides with salt and pepper. Heat the olive oil in a large, ovenproof skillet over medium-high heat. Add the pork and sear on all sides until the meat is golden. Transfer the pork to the oven and cook for about 35 minutes, or until the internal temperature reaches 145° F.

To prepare the cabbage or Swiss chard: Blanch the Savoy cabbage or Swiss chard leaves in boiling salted water for about 1 minute, or until slightly tender. Drain the leaves on paper towels and, if desired, use scissors to cut them into desired shapes (see photo).

To prepare the apples: Melt 2 tablespoons butter in a medium skillet over medium heat. Add the sugar and the apples and sauté them, stirring often, until the apples are tender, about 15 minutes.

SERVES 4

To make the sauce: While the pork loin is roasting, heat the olive oil in a medium skillet over medium-high heat. Add the diced pork and cook until it is golden brown. Stir in the onion, carrot, and celery. Cook, stirring often, for about 10 minutes, or until the vegetables are tender. Stir in the tomato paste and garlic; then add the wine, water and sugar, mixing well. Simmer the sauce for about 20 minutes; then strain it though a sieve. Return the sauce to the pan over low heat and whisk in the chilled butter. Season it to taste with salt and pepper. Keep warm.

To assemble and serve: Place one leaf of cabbage on each serving plate, and, if desired, wrap the stem with a curlicue of bacon. Slice the tenderloin into 1/2-inch thick slices and arrange 3 to 4 slices on top of each leaf. Drizzle the pork with the warm sauce. Using a large ice cream scoop, place one scoop of polenta on each plate. If desired, top the polenta with Crispy Fried Onions (see Recipe Index). Spoon the cooked apples alongside the pork.

SAUCE FOR PORK LOIN

2	tablespoons olive oil
1/2	cup diced pork
1	small onion, finely diced
1	small carrot, finely diced
1	stalk celery, finely diced
1	tablespoon tomato paste
2	garlic cloves, minced
1	cup dry white wine
1	cup water
1	tablespoon sugar
2	tablespoons butter, chilled and cut into 1/2-inch pieces

Salt and freshly ground black pepper to taste

PORK TENDERLOIN

24 ounces pork tenderloin

Salt and freshly ground black pepper
    to taste

3   tablespoons olive oil

1   tablespoons red curry paste

COCONUT CURRY SAUCE

1   13-ounce can unsweetened
    coconut milk

1/2 cup heavy cream

1/2 teaspoon red curry paste

Salt and freshly ground black pepper
    to taste

SERVES 4-6

PORK TENDERLOIN
COCONUT CURRY SAUCE

STEAMED JASMINE RICE AND SAUTÉED SNOW PEAS OR LONG BEANS ARE THE PERFECT ACCOMPANIMENTS FOR THIS DISH. LOOK FOR RED CURRY PASTE IN THE ASIAN SECTION OF YOUR LOCAL MARKET, OR AT SPECIALTY ASIAN GROCERS. POUR A CHILLED DRY RIESLING OR GEWÜRZTRAMINER TO MATCH THE SPICINESS OF THE RED CURRY SAUCE.

Preheat the oven to 350° F.

To prepare the pork tenderloin: Trim the fat from the pork tenderloin and sprinkle it liberally with kosher salt and pepper. Heat the olive oil in an ovenproof skillet over medium high heat and sear the pork on all sides until it is golden brown. Remove the pan from the heat and brush the pork with the red curry paste. Place the pork in the oven and roast for about 25 minutes, or until the internal temperature reaches 120° F. (rare).

To make the Coconut Curry Sauce: Combine the coconut milk, heavy cream, and remaining 1/2 teaspoon of red curry paste in a saucepan. Bring the mixture to a boil, then reduce the heat and simmer for about 15 minutes, or until the mixture is slightly thickened. Season to taste with salt and pepper.

To serve: When the pork is done, allow it to sit at room temperature for 3 minutes before slicing into 1/2-inch thick slices. Fan out on serving plates. Ladle about 2 tablespoons of the sauce over each serving of pork.

Pork Tenderloin
Sage & Mozzarella Stuffing

FILLED WITH A MOZZARELLA CHEESE STUFFING SEASONED WITH HERBS AND GARLIC, THIS IS A SIMPLE DISH TO PREPARE. IT IS WELL-PAIRED WITH A FRUITY RED WINE, SUCH AS A CHIANTI OR ZINFANDEL, OR A LUSCIOUS WHITE WINE SMACKING OF MINERALS, SUCH AS A WHITE BURGUNDY FROM FRANCE. POLENTA OR MASHED POTATOES AND A CRISP GREEN SALAD ROUND OUT THIS DISH NICELY.

Preheat the oven to 350° F.

Make a lengthwise slit down the center of the tenderloin and set it aside. Heat 3 tablespoons of olive oil in a medium skillet over medium heat. Stir in the shallots, minced garlic, celery and minced sage. Cook for about 10 minutes, or until the vegetables are tender. Place the vegetables in the refrigerator and cool to room temperature. When cool, blend in the drained mozzarella cheese to form a creamy mixture.

Stuff the mixture into the slit in the tenderloin, and tie the pork at 3-inch intervals with kitchen twine. Heat about 3 tablespoons of olive oil in a large ovenproof skillet. Sprinkle the pork with salt and freshly ground black pepper. Sear the pork on each side, and then place the pan in the oven. Bake for about 25 minutes, or until the pork reaches an internal temperature of 140° F (medium rare). Let the pork sit at room temperature for
3 minutes before slicing.

To serve: Remove the twine and slice into 1-inch slices.

24	ounces pork tenderloin, trimmed

Olive oil, as needed

2	shallots, minced
2	garlic cloves, minced
2	stalks celery, finely diced
10	fresh sage leaves, minced
12	ounces fresh mozzarella cheese, drained

Salt and freshly ground black pepper to taste

SERVES 4

Women of The Stephanie Inn:
STEPHANIE SNYDER

STEPHANIE MARTIN-SNYDER, FOR WHOM THE STEPHANIE INN IS NAMED, IS THE DAUGHTER OF JAN AND THE LATE STEVE MARTIN. WHEN STEPHANIE WAS JUST SEVEN YEARS OLD, HER PARENTS MOVED TO CANNON BEACH, WHERE THEY PURCHASED THEIR FIRST HOTEL, THE SURFSAND RESORT. WITH BOTH OF HER PARENTS WORKING IN THEIR HOTELS AND RESTAURANTS DAY AND NIGHT, STEPHANIE WAS RAISED WITH HOSPITALITY IN HER BLOOD. ACCORDING TO HER MOTHER, JAN MARTIN, STEPHANIE OFFICIALLY STARTED HER HOTEL CAREER AT THE AGE OF EIGHT—REMOVING LITTER FROM THE HOTEL PARKING LOT WITH A FIRE POKER. SHE WENT ON TO WORK IN ALL ASPECTS OF THE HOSPITALITY BUSINESS, WORKING IN LAUNDRY AND HOUSEKEEPING, AS A FRONT DESK CLERK, AND A WAITRESS, AMONG OTHERS. "STEPHANIE HAS LIVED AND BREATHED THE HOTEL BUSINESS SINCE SHE WAS BORN," SAYS HER MOTHER, JAN MARTIN. UPON GRADUATION FROM HIGH SCHOOL, STEPHANIE STUDIED HOTEL MANAGEMENT, AND, AFTER FURTHERING HER CAREER IN THE HOSPITALITY INDUSTRY, SHE EVENTUALLY RETURNED TO CANNON BEACH TO WORK FOR HER PARENTS' BUSINESS, AND TO HELP LAUNCH HER NAMESAKE HOTEL, THE STEPHANIE INN. STEPHANIE LIVES IN ARCH CAPE WITH HER HUSBAND, RYAN SNYDER (WHO ALSO WORKS FOR THE COMPANY), AND THEIR SON, STEPHEN, NAMED AFTER STEPHANIE'S FATHER, THE LATE STEVE MARTIN.

STEPHANIE'S BARBECUED LIME-CHICKEN FAJITAS

STEPHANIE LOVES TO COOK FOR FRIENDS AND FAMILY. SHE OFTEN HAS HELP FROM HER HUSBAND RYAN SNYDER. THIS IS ONE OF STEPHANIE'S FAVORITE RECIPES FOR MILD NIGHTS AT THE COAST WHEN YOU CAN BARBECUE OUTDOORS. SHE PREPARES THE LIME MARINADE IN THE MORNING AND LETS THE CHICKEN MARINATE ALL DAY, TURNING IT SEVERAL TIMES TO MARINATE BOTH SIDES BEFORE GRILLING. THIS DISH IS FOR AN INFORMAL MEAL, WHERE GUESTS ARE FREE TO LAYER THE INGREDIENTS HOWEVER THEY LIKE. STEPHANIE'S FAVORITE WINE TO SERVE WITH THIS SPICY DISH IS A CHILLED PINOT GRIS. A FROSTY MARGARITA IS ALSO WELCOME.

In a non–reactive baking pan, combine the chicken breasts with the garlic, oregano, chili powder, cilantro, and lime juice, mixing well. Let the chicken marinate for 4 to 8 hours, turning occasionally. Season with salt and freshly ground black pepper.

Preheat a charcoal or electric grill to medium heat. Using tongs or a slotted spoon, remove the chicken breasts from the marinade and place on the hot grill. Cook, turning several times, until the chicken is cooked through and the juices run clear when the chicken is pierced with a fork. Discard marinade.

Meanwhile, heat the olive oil in a large skillet over medium-high heat and sauté the peppers and onion, stirring often, until they are soft and golden on the edges, about 12 minutes. Remove the mixture from the heat and set aside.

Heat a dry skillet over medium heat and warm the tortillas on both sides. Keep the tortillas warm in a slow oven (250° F). Slice the chicken breasts into 1/2-inch-thick slices.

To serve: Set out the tortillas, chicken, sautéed peppers, lettuce, diced tomatoes, sliced avocados, black olives, cheese, salsa, sour cream, and fresh lime wedges so each guest can layer the ingredients however they like.

6	6-ounce boneless chicken breasts (approximately), with or without skin according to taste
4	garlic cloves, minced
1	tablespoon fresh oregano, minced
1	tablespoon chili powder
1/2	cup chopped fresh cilantro
	Juice of 6 fresh limes
	Salt and freshly ground black pepper to taste
3	tablespoons olive oil
1	each red, yellow and green pepper, cored, seeded and cut into 1-inch pieces
1	Walla Walla onion, or other sweet onion, diced
8	corn or flour tortillas (approximately)
4	cups fresh romaine or iceberg lettuce, shredded
2	tomatoes, diced
2	avocados, sliced
1	cup sliced black olives
3	cups grated sharp cheddar cheese
	Salsa, as needed
	Sour cream, as needed
	Fresh lime wedges

SERVES 4 TO 6

4 cups fresh baby spinach leaves

Salt and freshly ground black pepper to taste

Ground nutmeg to taste

4 6- to 8-ounce boneless chicken breasts, skin-on, trimmed, rinsed and patted dry

Salt and freshly ground black pepper to taste

2 tablespoons canola or safflower oil

1/2 cup toasted almonds, sliced

2 tablespoons butter, softened

1/4 cup Gorgonzola cheese, or heavily veined blue cheese, crumbled

2 tablespoons honey

Toasted almonds for garnish

SERVES 4

CHICKEN BREASTS
GORGONZOLA & SPINACH STUFFING

STUFFED WITH ZESTY GORGONZOLA CHEESE, FRESH SPINACH AND SLICED ALMONDS, THESE TENDER CHICKEN BREASTS ARE BEAUTIFULLY MATCHED WITH A SPICY ZINFANDEL OR RHONE WINE. SERVE THEM WITH CREAMY POLENTA (SEE RECIPE INDEX) AND SAUTÉED GREEN BEANS.

Preheat the oven to 375° F.

To prepare the spinach: Rinse the spinach leaves in several changes of water, until clean. Place the wet spinach leaves in a large kettle over medium-high heat and cook, stirring constantly, for about 3 minutes, or until the leaves are slightly wilted and still bright green. Rinse leaves immediately under cold running water to stop cooking. When the leaves are cool, shake or spin them dry. Place them in a clean bowl and season them with salt, pepper, and nutmeg.

To prepare the chicken breasts: Season the prepared chicken breasts with salt and pepper. Heat the oil in a heavy skillet over medium-high heat, and sauté the chicken breasts, skin-side-up, until they are golden brown. Remove the chicken breasts from the heat and let them cool for about 15 minutes, or until cool enough to handle.

To prepare the stuffing: Meanwhile, coarsely chop the almonds and place in a large bowl. Stir in the softened butter, crumbled cheese, and honey, mixing well. Coarsely chop the spinach and add it to the cheese mixture. Season the mixture to taste with salt and pepper.

To complete the dish: Slice a deep pocket into the thickest part of each chicken breast, being careful not to cut all the way through. Stuff each chicken breast with 1/4 of the cheese and spinach mixture.

Place the stuffed chicken breasts in a baking pan, skin side up and place in the preheated oven. Roast for about 25 minutes, or until the juices run clear when breasts are pierced with a knife.

To serve: Slice each breast diagonally into 3 pieces and fan out on serving plates.

CRISPY SKINNED DUCK BREASTS
HUCKLEBERRY PORT SAUCE

IN LATE SUMMER, NORTHWEST FORESTS ARE FILLED WITH WILD HUCKLE-BERRIES—BOTH THE BLUE AND RED VARIETIES. FRESH OR DRIED BLUEBERRIES CAN BE SUBSTITUTED IN THE SAUCE. SERVE THE DUCK WITH LENTILS COOKED WITH PEPPER BACON, ALONG WITH ROASTED SLABS OF FENNEL BULB SEASONED WITH SALT, PEPPER, AND OLIVE OIL. THIS DISH WARRANTS A DEEPLY FLAVORED, SPICY RED WINE, SUCH AS A CABERNET SAUVIGNON, SYRAH, OR MERLOT.

Preheat the oven to 250° F.

To prepare the duck: With a sharp knife, slice the skin of the duck breasts about 1/4-inch deep at 1/2-inch intervals on each side. Season the breasts with salt and pepper. Heat the oil in a large, ovenproof skillet over medium-high heat, and sear the duck breasts, skin side down, until they are golden and crispy. Turn the heat to low, flip the duck breasts over and cook about 3 to 5 minutes, or until they are cooked to desired doneness, about 3 minutes for medium rare. Remove the duck breasts from the roasting pan and set them on a clean baking pan. Keep the duck warm in the oven.

To make the Huckleberry Port Sauce: Pour off the excess fat. Place reserved 1/4 cup of pan juices in a saucepan and bring to a boil over medium-high heat. Stir in the port and huckleberries and continue to simmer the mixture rapidly until it is reduced by one-half and is thick and syrupy, about 12 minutes. Remove the sauce from the heat and whisk in the chilled butter, one tablespoon at a time. Season the sauce to taste with salt and pepper, and cover to keep warm.

To serve: Allow the duck breasts to rest at room temperature for 2 minutes. Slice each breast into 6 to 8 slices. Fan out the slices on serving plates and drizzle with Huckleberry Port Sauce.

CHEF'S TIP

If you are buying whole ducks for this recipe, save the legs for Duck Confit, the recipe that follows on the next page.

4	6-ounce duck breasts, skin on, deboned
	Salt and freshly ground black pepper to taste
2	tablespoons olive oil

HUCKLEBERRY PORT SAUCE

1/4	cup reserved pan drippings from the duck
1	cup port wine
2	cups huckleberries, blueberries or blackberries
4	tablespoons (1/2 stick) butter, chilled
	Salt and freshly ground black pepper to taste

SERVES 4

Duck Confit

6   duck legs, skin on

2   bay leaves

8   juniper berries

2   bunches fresh thyme,
    de-stemmed

1/2 cup chopped fresh parsley

4   garlic cloves, peeled

2   teaspoons black peppercorns

2   tablespoons kosher salt

Approximately 8 cups rendered
    duck fat (enough to cover
    the legs by 1-inch)

Rubbed with fragrant spices and simmered long and slow in rendered duck fat, this dish simply melts in your mouth. Serve the confit with roasted root vegetables, such as beets, rutabagas and carrots, and pour a rich, spicy Pinot Noir. Stephanie Inn chefs often serve the duck legs with cooked lentils and roasted new potatoes, which nicely balance the richness of the duck. Look for prepared rendered duck fat at Asian markets or specialty stores, or ask you grocer to order it for you. Plan ahead, as the duck should marinate for 24 hours.

Rinse the duck legs and pat them dry on paper towels. Meanwhile, combine the bay leaves, juniper berries, thyme, parsley, garlic and peppercorns in a food processor or blender. Process the mixture at high speed until it is coarsely ground, scraping down the sides of the bowl as necessary. Transfer the spices to a bowl and mix in the kosher salt. Rub the duck legs liberally with the spices; then place the legs in a large baking pan (large enough so that they don't overlap). Cover the duck with plastic wrap; then place another baking sheet, weighted with something heavy, such as rocks or bricks, over the duck legs. Place the duck in the refrigerator for 24 hours.

The following day, remove the duck legs from the refrigerator and lightly brush away excess dry rub. Heat the duck fat in a large skillet over medium heat until it reaches a simmer and then carefully add the legs to the fat. Return the heat to a simmer and cook for about 2 hours, or until the meat is very tender when pierced with a knife.

Just before serving, remove the duck legs from the fat, and wipe them lightly with paper towels to remove excess fat. Heat a non-stick skillet over medium-low heat. Place the legs, skin-side-down in the skillet and cook them for about 10 minutes on each side, or until they are warmed through.

To serve: Serve warm with a fresh green salad and roasted new potatoes.

Chef's Tip

Once cooked, the finished duck legs can be stored in the duck fat, covered in the refrigerator, for at least one week.

Serves 6

Slow-Roasted Veal Shanks (Osso Bucco)
Orange-Rosemary Sauce & Gremolata

For a hearty fall or winter dish, serve these veal shanks with the simmered root vegetables plus a mixture of hearty greens sautéed in olive oil. Kale, Swiss chard, mustard greens, and spinach are excellent choices. Gremolata, a flavorful garnish made with minced parsley, lemon zest, and garlic, adds the perfect touch to this meltingly tender dish. Pour a big, voluptuous red wine such as a cabernet sauvignon, merlot, or aged Burgundy to match the hearty flavors in this dish.

Preheat the oven to 325° F.

Season the veal shanks liberally with salt and pepper. Heat the olive oil in a large, ovenproof stockpot over medium-high heat and sear the shanks on both sides, until they are golden. Remove the shanks from the pot and set aside. Reduce the heat to medium. Add more olive oil to the pot, as necessary, then stir in the celery, onion, carrots, shallots, and garlic. Cook, stirring often, until the vegetables are tender, about 10 minutes. Stir in the orange juice, red wine, lemon zest, rosemary, parsley, and thyme. Return the shanks to the pan, adding water, as necessary, to cover them.

Place the veal in the oven and cook for about 3 hours, basting occasionally, until the meat is falling off the bone. Transfer the shanks to a baking pan and keep warm in a low oven (200° F.)

Pour half of the cooking juices into a smaller saucepan and bring to a boil over high heat. Reduce the heat to a rapid simmer, and cook until the sauce is slightly thickened, about 12 minutes. Remove the rosemary and thyme sprigs before serving.

To make the Gremolata: In a small bowl, mix together the minced parsley, lemon zest, and garlic until combined.

To serve: Distribute the sautéed greens in six large serving bowls. Top with a veal shank and ladle the warm sauce liberally over the meat. Top with a spoonful of Gremolata.

6	12- to 14-ounce veal or lamb shanks
	Kosher salt and freshly ground black pepper to taste
3	tablespoons olive oil
2	stalks celery, cut into 1-inch pieces
1	large onion, cut into 1-inch pieces
2	large carrots, cut into 1-inch pieces
6	shallots, roughly chopped
4	garlic cloves, minced
2	cups orange juice
2	cups dry red wine
	Zest of 1 lemon
2	sprigs fresh rosemary (about 3-inches long)
1/4	cup chopped fresh parsley
2	sprigs fresh thyme
3	cups mixed hearty greens, cleaned and sautéed in 2 tablespoons olive oil

GREMOLATA:

1/2	cup minced fresh parsley
	Zest of one lemon
1	garlic clove, minced

SERVES 6

New York Striploin Steak
Parsley Oil & Veal Stock Reduction

6 pounds whole New York striploin steak, trimmed of fat and sinew

Salt and freshly ground black pepper to taste

1/4 cup canola oil

Veal Stock Reduction (Demi-Glace)
see Recipe Index and
Chef's Tip below

Parsley Oil
see Recipe Index

THIS IS A GREAT WAY TO COOK NEW YORK STEAKS! (CALL YOUR BUTCHER OR GROCER AHEAD TO ORDER THIS CUT OF MEAT). THE MEAT IS SO MOIST AND FLAVORFUL THAT IT'S DIFFICULT TO RESIST. THE STEPHANIE INN CHEFS OFTEN SERVE IT WITH A VEAL-STOCK REDUCTION SAUCE (DEMI-GLACE) AND PARSLEY OIL DRIZZLED ON THE SIDE. YOUR FAVORITE BARBECUE SAUCE WOULD ALSO BE WONDERFUL. A BIG, FULL-BODIED RED WINE, SUCH AS A CABERNET SAUVIGNON OR MERLOT IS DEFINITELY IN ORDER. AU GRATIN GOLD POTATOES (SEE RECIPE INDEX) ARE A WELCOME COMPLEMENT.

Preheat the oven to 375° F.

Season the beef liberally with kosher salt and white pepper. Heat the canola oil in a large, heavy-bottomed skillet over medium-high heat. Add the meat to the hot oil and sear it for about 2 minutes on each side, or until golden brown. Place the seared beef on a baking sheet in the preheated oven and roast for about 10 to 15 minutes or until a meat thermometer registers 125° F (medium rare) or desired doneness.

To serve: Allow the beef to sit at room temperature for at least 5 minutes and then slice into 3/4 inch-thick slices. Place the beef slices on pre-warmed plates. Drizzle approximately 2 tablespoons of warm veal reduction sauce around each serving of beef, and then drizzle each plate with 1 tablespoon of parsley oil.

SERVES 6 TO 8

Chef's Tip

If you don't have time to make veal stock and reduce it—a time-consuming process to be sure—reduced veal stock (demi-glace) is available at most fine food stores or through many mail-order food companies.

Pairing Food and Wine

WINE HAS BEEN CALLED NATURE'S PERFECT CONDIMENT. WINE KEEPS THE
PALATE REFRESHED THROUGHOUT THE MEAL. WHILE THERE ARE NO ABSOLUTE
RULES REGARDING MATCHING FOOD AND WINE, THERE ARE DEFINITE REASONS
WHY SOME WINES TASTE BETTER WITH CERTAIN FOODS.

Our palates perceive certain flavors and textures in foods. These include salt, sugar,
acid, fat, and bitter flavors. Similarly, a wine's flavors and texture are perceived as
sugar, acid, fruit, tannin, and alcohol. When wine meets food on our palates, these
components combine in a number of ways, creating many different taste sensations.
Traditionally, mild meats and seafood are paired with white wine and heavier meats
are paired with full-bodied red wines.

Many wonderful things can happen when you drink wine with food. Wine can echo or
enhance the flavors and textures of a dish. For example, a supple Merlot brimming
with rich, ripe cherry flavors will magnify the rich flavor and succulent texture of
The Stephanie Inn's Crispy Skinned Duck Breasts with Dried Cherry Port Sauce.
Wine can also provide a contrast to the flavors of the food, providing a palate-
cleansing effect for rich or spicy dishes. The refreshing, cucumber-crisp acids of a
Sauvignon Blanc will slice right through the rich flavors of plump, briny oysters. The
astringent tannins in a full-bodied Cabernet Sauvignon will keep the palate refreshed
between rich bites of The Stephanie Inn's succulent New York Striploin Steak.

In the best of pairings, wine and food interact perfectly on the palate in a combination
of contrast and similarity, creating a sum greater than the parts. For example, the
crisp acids and lively fruit of a Semillon or Sauvignon Blanc will cut through the heat
of The Stephanie Inn's spicy Coconut Curried Prawns. The bright fruit flavors of the
wine complement the sweet, sea flavors of the seafood. The velvety texture and dark
cherry fruit of a full-bodied Merlot enhance tender, earthy-flavored lamb, while the
astringent tannins in the wine cut the richness of the lamb.

Theories aside, the most important thing to remember is: Drink the wine you like
best with the food you like best. In a restaurant turn to your wine steward to suggest
the wines which will enhance the dishes you have chosen for your meal.

White Wines with Food

For the most part, white wine is made from white grapes. Some white wines have a hint of sweetness, with pure, fresh flavors and crisp acids. Others are dry and crisp with no oak character. Fuller bodied white wines are dry and richly flavored, often laced with flavors of toast and vanilla from oak aging.

DELICATE WHITES, including Riesling, Gewürztraminer, and Chenin Blanc are typically aged in temperature-controlled stainless steel, which showcases the wine's inviting fresh fruit flavors and crisp acids. Some, including Johannesburg Riesling and Gewürztraminer, have a touch of sweetness. Others, such as dry Riesling, leave the barest impression of sweet fruit. Traditionally, these varietals are matched with lighter meats, such as veal, pork, chicken, and turkey. With their mouthwatering flavors of fruit and spice, they are also delicious matched with spicy Asian foods and with smoky, salty foods, such as cured meats and smoked seafood.

FULL-BODIED WHITES, including Semillon, Sauvignon Blanc, Pinot Gris, and Chardonnay, are beautifully balanced with deep, rich fruit and lively acids. Oak aging adds luscious notes of toast, spice, butter, and vanilla to these wines. With their lemony-crisp acids and delicate fruit, Semillon and Sauvignon Blanc make delicious partners for shellfish and other seafood. These varietals also marry well with lighter meats and poultry. Oak-aged Pinot Gris and Chardonnay have a rich, creamy texture and complex fruit flavors. These richer varietals hold up to more complex dishes. Some great matches include pork, pheasant, salmon, wild Chanterelle mushrooms, and dishes with rich cream sauces.

RED WINES WITH FOOD

LIGHTER REDS, such as some Pinot Noir, Chianti, and Beaujolais are versatile
wines that easily cross over into food territories once reserved for white wines.
With refreshing acids, vigorous fruit flavors laced with leather and cedar, and a silky
texture, these lighter reds are delicious with succulent braised meats including rabbit
and roast chicken. Other favorites include pasta, duck and lamb. Highlight the earthy
sweetness of vegetable dishes, especially those made with eggplant or potatoes, with
any of these varietals. Thanks to their refreshing acidity, lighter red wines also pair
nicely with full-flavored fish, including salmon, tuna and swordfish.

FULL-BODIED REDS, including Merlot, Cabernet Sauvignon, Cabernet Franc and
Syrah are packed with rich, ripe fruit, balanced by refreshing tannins and notes of
spice and vanilla from barrel fermentation. These robust reds hold up well to full-
flavored meats including lamb and beef, and especially with the toasty quality of
grilled meats.

APPETIZERS

Forest Winter Mushrooms
garlic, chives & Pecorino cheese

North Coast Clam Fritters
cocktail & tartar sauce

Painted Hills Tenderloin Crostini
dried cherries & garden beets

WINE: CHAMPAGNE DUVAL-LEROY NV

FIRST COURSE

Oregon Dungeness Crab Cake
organic greens,
white Balsamic vinegar & lemon

WINE: LAVELLE RIESLING 2000

SECOND COURSE

Pinot Gris Poached Salmon
arugula & creamy onions

WINE: CHEHALEM PINOT GRIS 2001

ENTRÉE

Lamb Rack
Oregon truffles, Nehalem Bay potatoes,
carrots & pinot jus

WINE: LAUREL HOOD PINOT NOIR 1999

CHEESE COURSE

*Selection of Oregon Cheeses,
including Tillamook, Oregon Blue,
& Bandon Cheddar*

WINE: EUGENE WINE CELLARS SYRAH 2000

DESSERT

Chocolate Hazelnut Torte
pear-blueberry parfait

A CELEBRATION OF JAMES BEARD'S BIRTHPLACE —
ONE HUNDRED YEARS LATER

IN JANUARY 2003, STEPHANIE INN EXECUTIVE CHEF JOHN NEWMAN WAS HONORED AS THE FIRST OF TWELVE OREGON CHEFS INVITED TO PREPARE A MEAL AT THE JAMES BEARD HOUSE IN GREENWICH VILLAGE, NEW YORK. THE EVENT WAS TO COMMEMORATE THE HUNDRED-YEAR ANNIVERSARY OF JAMES BEARD'S BIRTH, AND TO CELEBRATE HIS BIRTHPLACE—OREGON.

Less than two centuries after the native people had almost disappeared from the region, James Beard, one of America's most loved and respected culinary authorities, spent much of his life on the Oregon Coast. A painting on the cover of his autobiography, published in 1964, depicts Beard seated near the current location of The Stephanie Inn at a table on the seashore facing Tillamook Head and the sea. "Those busy days on the Oregon coast left their mark on me, and no place on earth, with the exception of Paris, has done as much to influence my professional life," he wrote.

The same foods utilized by the native coastal people—salmon, halibut, clams, crab, wild berries and mushrooms, to name a few—are still widely available. Modern chefs, beginning with James Beard, are preparing them in amazing ways, utilizing new cooking techniques, spices and a fusion of innovative ideas. The chefs at The Stephanie Inn are no exception.

In celebration of James Beard's birthday and birthplace, The Stephanie Inn chefs prepared the following menu, receiving rave reviews from guests and food writers across the country. The menu featured organically grown produce from King Fisher Farms in Nehalem, Oregon and a Pinot Noir from Cannon Beach winemaker, Laurel Hood.

ROASTED GARLIC CLOVES

1   whole garlic bulb

1   tablespoon olive oil

Salt and freshly ground black pepper
to taste

FRESH TOMATO SAUCE

3   medium tomatoes

2   garlic cloves, minced

1/4 cup tomato juice

4   leaves fresh basil,
finely shredded

Salt and freshly ground black pepper
to taste

PASTA

2 to 3 cups cooked pasta
(orecchiette, elbow
macaroni, or penne)

1/4 cup olive oil, or to taste

2   tablespoons butter

1   medium tomato, diced

3   tablespoons diced
sundried tomatoes in oil

10 Kalamata olives,
pitted and diced

3   leaves fresh basil,
finely shredded

Salt and freshly ground black pepper
to taste

1   cup freshly grated Pecorino or
Parmesan cheese

PASTA
ROASTED GARLIC, HEIRLOOM TOMATOES, BASIL, KALAMATA OLIVES & PECORINO CHEESE

ROBUSTLY FLAVORED WITH ROASTED GARLIC, KALAMATA OLIVES AND PECORINO CHEESE, THIS PASTA CAN BE SERVED AS A SIDE DISH OR A VEGETARIAN ENTRÉE. THE ROASTED GARLIC AND FRESH TOMATO SAUCE CAN BE PREPARED SEVERAL HOURS AHEAD. POUR A MEDIUM-BODIED RED, SUCH AS A CHIANTI OR PINOT NOIR.

To prepare the Roasted Garlic Cloves: Preheat the oven to 325° F. Slice about 1/4-inch off the pointed end of the garlic bulb. Place the garlic bulb in a baking dish, cut-side up. Drizzle with olive oil and sprinkle with salt and pepper. Bake for about 30 minutes, or until the garlic is tender when pierced with a fork. Let the garlic cool until it can be handled, then split the cloves apart and remove their papery covering. Set them aside.

To prepare the Fresh Tomato Sauce: Trim the tops from the tomatoes and place the tomatoes in a blender or food processor with the garlic and tomato juice. Purée the mixture and transfer it to a clean bowl. Stir in the shredded basil and season to taste with salt and pepper.

To assemble and serve: In a large mixing bowl, toss the cooked pasta with the olive oil and butter. Stir in the roasted garlic cloves, diced tomatoes, sundried tomatoes, olives, and basil. Season to taste with salt and pepper. Spoon the pasta into pre-warmed bowls and top with the tomato sauce and grated cheese.

SERVES 2

4   large Yukon Gold potatoes
    (or other new potatoes),
    unpeeled

2   large parsnips, peeled and
    trimmed

3   tablespoons butter, chilled and
    cut into small pieces

1/2 cup heavy cream
    (approximately)

4   ounces soft goat cheese

3   tablespoons chopped chives

Salt and freshly ground black pepper
    to taste

Chopped chives for garnish

SERVES 4

MASHED POTATOES & PARSNIPS
GOAT CHEESE

PARSNIPS AND GOAT CHEESE ADD A ZESTY FLAVOR TO MASHED POTATOES.
SERVE THESE WITH ANY OF YOUR FAVORITE MEAT, POULTRY, OR SEAFOOD.

Dice the potatoes and parsnips into 1/2" pieces, place in a large kettle, and cover with salted water. Bring the water to a boil over high heat, then reduce the heat and simmer until the potatoes and parships are very tender when pierced with a fork, about 20 minutes.

Drain the potatoes and parsnips and place them in a large mixing bowl. Using a potato masher, mash the potatoes and parsnips until they are fairly smooth. Whisk in the butter, cream, goat cheese and chives. Season to taste with salt and pepper. Garnish with additional chopped chives

6   large Yukon Gold or new red
    potatoes, thinly sliced

3   cups heavy cream

1   cup grated Asiago or
    Parmesan cheese

1   teaspoon grated nutmeg

Salt and freshly ground black pepper
    to taste

SERVES 6

AU GRATIN GOLD POTATOES

RICH AND EARTHY, THESE ARE GOOD WITH JUST ABOUT ANYTHING, ESPECIALLY
BEEF, LAMB, PORK, OR SALMON.

Preheat the oven to 325° F.

Grease a 9" x 11" casserole dish.

In a large bowl, mix together the potatoes, cream, grated cheese and nutmeg. Season to taste with salt and pepper. Turn the potatoes into the prepared pan; cover with aluminum foil and bake for about 1½ hours, or until the potatoes are almost cooked through.

Remove the foil and bake for about 30 minutes more, or until the top is bubbling and golden.

CRISPY POTATOES
GOAT CHEESE STUFFING

AFTER SCOOPING OUT THE INSIDES OF THE POTATOES, THE STEPHANIE INN CHEFS DEEP-FRY THE SKINS AND TOPS OF THE POTATOES, THEN FILL THEM WITH CREAMY MASHED POTATOES MIXED WITH CHEESE AND HERBS. IF YOU WISH, YOU CAN FORGO THE DEEP-FRYING AND SIMPLY BAKE THE STUFFED POTATOES. THESE ARE DELICIOUS SERVED WITH GRILLED STEAKS OR SEAFOOD.

Preheat the oven to 375° F.

Place the potatoes on a baking sheet and brush with olive oil to coat thoroughly. Roast the potatoes until they are tender when pierced with a fork. Let the potatoes cool slightly and then slice off the top of each potato (about 3/8-inch). Using a small spoon, scrape the center of the potatoes into a mixing bowl, being careful not to break the skins.

In a heavy-bottomed skillet or deep fat fryer, heat 3 inches of peanut oil to 350° F. When the oil is hot, use tongs to place the potato skin and tops in the oil. Fry until they are golden, then remove from the hot oil and drain on paper towels.

Reduce the oven heat to 350° F. Mash the potatoes with a potato masher, adding heavy cream as necessary so they reach a firm, but creamy consistency. Stir in the goat cheese, chives, parsley, and grated cheese. Season to taste with cayenne pepper, salt and pepper. Fill the fried potato skins with the mashed potatoes and top with the crisp tops. Place the potatoes on a baking sheet and bake for about 20 minutes, or until heated through. Sprinkle the tops with chopped chives for garnish.

4   large Yukon Gold potatoes or other new potatoes

Olive oil, as needed

Peanut or canola oil, as needed for deep-fat frying

Heavy cream, as needed

2   ounces soft goat cheese

1   tablespoon chives, chopped

1   tablespoon parsley, chopped

3/4 cup grated Parmesan cheese

Pinch of cayenne pepper

Salt and freshly ground black pepper to taste

Chopped chives for garnish

SERVES 4

Women of The Stephanie Inn:
Jan Martin

JANICE KAY MARTIN (BORN JANICE SCHLABACH) WAS RAISED ON A NORTH DAKOTA FARM, WHERE SHE LIVED WITH HER FAMILY (HER PARENTS, A BROTHER, AND FIVE OLDER SISTERS) IN THE DAYS FOLLOWING THE END OF WORLD WAR II. FOLLOWING HER MARRIAGE TO STEVE MARTIN, IN 1967, THE COUPLE PURCHASED THEIR FIRST HOTEL IN CANNON BEACH, OREGON, AND IN THE YEARS FOLLOWING, THEY PURCHASED A NUMBER OF PROPERTIES, INCLUDING THE OCEANFRONT PROPERTY IN CANNON BEACH THAT WOULD BECOME THE STEPHANIE INN. DURING HER MANY YEARS OF WORK IN THE HOSPITALITY BUSINESS, JAN HAS WORKED HANDS-ON IN EVERY DEPARTMENT. HER GRACIOUSNESS, COMMITMENT TO HER FAMILY, FRIENDS, AND EMPLOYEES, AND HER PHILOSOPHY OF TREATING EACH VISITOR AS A GUEST IN HER OWN HOME, HAVE MADE HER ONE OF THE MOST RESPECTED WOMEN IN THE HOSPITALITY BUSINESS.

Jan Martin's Broccoli Casserole
Pimiento & Slivered Almonds

THIS FLAVORFUL DISH IS A FAVORITE JAN LOVES TO PREPARE FOR ENTERTAINING AND FAMILY GATHERINGS.

Preheat the oven to 350° F.

Grease a 9" x 11" casserole dish.

Slice or break the broccoli heads into lengthwise pieces. Place the broccoli florets in a kettle and cover with salted water. Bring the water to a boil over high heat, then reduce the heat to a simmer and cook until the broccoli is tender when pierced with a fork, about 5 minutes. Drain the broccoli in a colander and spoon it into the prepared casserole dish.

In a mixing bowl, combine the mayonnaise, lemon juice, grated cheese, mushroom soup, and 1/4 cup water, mixing well. Pour the mixture over the broccoli. Top the casserole with the Cheez-it cracker crumbs, chopped pimientos, and slivered almonds. Cover the casserole dish with aluminum foil and bake about 25 minutes. Remove the foil and continue cooking for about 10 minutes or until the topping is golden brown.

3	pounds fresh broccoli, rinsed, stems trimmed
1/2	cup mayonnaise
1	tablespoon fresh lemon juice
1	cup grated sharp cheddar cheese
1	can cream of mushroom soup
1/4	cup water
1	cup Cheez-it® cracker crumbs
1	cup chopped pimientos
1/2	cup slivered almonds

SERVES 6 TO 8

BARLEY RISOTTO
FRESH HERBS & PARMESAN CHEESE

NUTTY AND CHEWY, BARLEY MAKES A FLAVORFUL ALTERNATIVE TO THE RICE TRADITIONALLY USED IN RISOTTOS. SERVE THIS CREAMY SIDE DISH WITH PORK, SEAFOOD OR POULTRY.

1/4 cup olive oil

2 shallots, minced

1 garlic clove, minced

3/4 cup pearl barley

1/4 cup dry white wine

3 cups hot water (approximately)

2 tablespoons finely sliced fresh basil

2 tablespoons minced fresh parsley

1/2 cup grated Parmesan cheese

Salt and freshly ground black pepper to taste

Heat the olive oil over medium heat in a large, heavy-bottomed kettle. Stir in the shallots and minced garlic. Cook about 3 minutes, or until the vegetables are soft. Add the barley, stirring constantly, and sauté for about 2 minutes to coat all the grains. Stir in the wine, and simmer until the wine has nearly evaporated. Add 1 cup of water and reduce the heat to medium low. Stirring often, cook until the barley has absorbed the water. Add another cup of water. Repeat this process until the barley has softened and nearly all of the water has been absorbed. Stir in the fresh herbs and cheese and season to taste with salt and pepper.

SERVES 4

CREAMY POLENTA

IF DESIRED, ADD SAUTÉED ONION, GARLIC AND SPINACH TO THIS CREAMY DISH. FOR A SPECIAL TREAT, SUBSTITUTE BLUE CHEESE FOR THE PARMESAN CHEESE.

Combine the water, cream, and salt in a large, heavy-bottomed kettle. Bring the mixture to a boil over high heat, and then reduce the heat to a simmer. Stirring constantly with a wooden spoon, gradually add the cornmeal in a slow steady stream. Cook the mixture at a very low simmer, stirring constantly for about 10 minutes. As the polenta cooks, it will thicken and eventually pull away from the sides of the pan. When it does, remove the pan from the heat and whisk in the butter and grated cheese. Season to taste with salt and pepper.

2	cups water
1	cup heavy cream
2	teaspoons salt
1½	cups polenta (coarse ground yellow cornmeal)
3	tablespoons butter, softened
1/2	cup Parmesan or Asiago cheese

Salt and freshly ground black pepper to taste

SERVES 4-6

GRILLED ASPARAGUS SPEARS

2   pounds fresh asparagus,
     rinsed and stems trimmed

3   tablespoons olive oil,
     or as needed

Salt and freshly ground pepper
     to taste

GRILLING ASPARAGUS BRINGS OUT A WONDERFUL NUTTY FLAVOR. THIS MAKES A DELICIOUS, SIMPLE ACCOMPANIMENT TO ANY MEAL. LOOK FOR SLENDER STALKS OF ASPARAGUS, THE FRESHER THE BETTER.

Preheat a barbecue or electric grill. Toss the asparagus spears with olive oil and season them with salt and pepper. Place the spears on the hot grill and cook for about 2 minutes on each side, or until they are lightly charred.

SERVES 4

GARLICKY SAUTÉED MUSHROOMS

SIMMERED IN RED WINE, GARLIC, SOY SAUCE, AND HERBS, THIS TASTY MUSHROOM SIDE DISH IS THE ULTIMATE COMPANION FOR GRILLED STEAKS OR SEAFOOD.

Heat the olive oil in a large skillet over medium-high heat. Stir in the garlic and shallots, and cook for about 1 to 2 minutes, or until they are slightly golden. Stir in the mushrooms and cook, stirring often, for about 5 minutes. Stir in the soy sauce and red wine. Reduce the heat and simmer the mushrooms for about 15 minutes, or until they are softened. Add the chopped chives and parsley, and season to taste with salt and pepper.

2   tablespoons olive oil

2   garlic cloves, minced

2   shallots, minced

3   cups button mushrooms (white or brown), wiped clean and stems removed

1   tablespoon soy sauce

1/2   bunch chives, finely chopped

1/2   bunch fresh parsley, finely chopped

Salt and freshly ground black pepper to taste

SERVES 6

1 large onion, roughly chopped

1 carrot, diced in 1-inch pieces

2 tomatoes, diced

2 celery stalks, diced in 1-inch pieces

2 garlic cloves, minced

1 bay leaf

2 teaspoons black peppercorns

1 sprig fresh thyme

1 bunch fresh parsley

5 button or crimini mushrooms, wiped clean

4 cups cold water

1/2 cup dry white wine

Salt to taste

MAKES ABOUT 1 QUART

VEGETABLE STOCK

THIS MAKES A GREAT SUBSTITUTE FOR CHICKEN STOCK IN VEGETARIAN SOUPS OR SAUCES.

Combine all the ingredients in a large stockpot and bring to a boil over high heat. Reduce the heat to a simmer and cook for 30 minutes, stirring occasionally. Strain the stock through a fine sieve and add salt to taste.

FISH STOCK VARIATION

LIGHT, FLAVORFUL FISH STOCK IS A PERFECT INGREDIENT IN SAUCES MADE FOR WHITE FISH AND SEAFOOD DISHES. TRY IT IN PESTO CREAM SAUCE SERVED WITH SEARED HALIBUT FILLETS (SEE RECIPE INDEX).

To make Fish Stock, follow the recipe for Vegetable Stock, but replace the carrots and tomatoes with 1 cup of bones from a white fish such as halibut or cod, or 1 cup of shrimp shells.

Veal Stock

You'll find any number of ways to make use of this tasty stock, which will keep up to one week in the refrigerator. It can also be divided into smaller portions and frozen in self-sealing plastic bags for future use.

Preheat the oven to 400° F.

Spread the veal bones, onions, carrots, and celery on a baking pan. Roast the bones and vegetables for about 1 hour, until they are evenly browned, turning occasionally. Let the bones and vegetables cool to room temperature. Transfer the ingredients to a large stockpot; add the bouquet garni, garlic, tomato paste, wine, and cold water. The water should stand 4 inches above the bones. Bring the mixture to a boil. Reduce the heat to a low simmer and cook for about 6 hours, occasionally skimming off and discarding any fat or froth that floats to the surface. Strain, cool, and refrigerate.

2½ pounds veal knucklebones

2 medium onions, halved

2 medium carrots, roughly chopped

2 stalks celery

1 bouquet garni:
2 tablespoons each of thyme, bay leaf, black peppercorns, and parsley, tied in cheesecloth

10 cloves of garlic

2 tablespoons tomato paste

2 cups red wine

12 cups cold water, or as needed

MAKES ABOUT 2 QUARTS

Veal Stock Reduction (Demi-Glace)

The chefs at The Stephanie Inn often reduce a portion of veal stock to a syrup known as demi-glace and serve it as a warm sauce with meat dishes

Bring 2 cups of veal stock to a boil in a skillet over medium-high heat. Simmer until the sauce is reduced to a syrup-like consistency.

MAKES ABOUT 1 / 2 CUP

PEPPERCORN CREAM SAUCE

2   tablespoons olive oil

2   garlic cloves, minced

1   shallot, minced

2   tablespoons black peppercorns

1   bay leaf

1/2 cup dry white wine

2   cups heavy cream

Salt to taste

MAKES ABOUT 1 CUP

SERVE THIS PEPPERY SAUCE WITH GRILLED SEAFOOD, INCLUDING HALIBUT OR STURGEON, OR WITH GRILLED FILET MIGNON. THE CHEFS AT THE STEPHANIE INN RECOMMEND 1 OUNCE (2 TABLESPOONS) OF SAUCE FOR EVERY 4 OUNCES OF FISH OR MEAT.

Heat the olive oil in a saucepan over medium heat. Stir in the garlic, shallot, peppercorns and bay leaf. Cook the mixture for about 10 minutes, or until the shallots are soft. Stir in the white wine and simmer, stirring often, until the mixture has reduced by one-half. Add the heavy cream and simmer until the sauce has thickened, about 20 minutes. Strain the sauce through a sieve and season to taste with salt.

PESTO

2   cups fresh basil leaves (or other herbs), stems removed

1   cup fresh parsley, stems removed

2   garlic cloves, minced

Juice of one fresh lemon

1/4 cup pine nuts (or other nuts), toasted

1/4 cup grated Asiago or Parmesan cheese

1½   cups olive oil

Salt and freshly ground black pepper to taste

MAKES ABOUT 2 CUPS

THE STEPHANIE INN CHEFS OFTEN SUBSTITUTE DIFFERENT HERBS FOR THE BASIL IN THIS VERSATILE SAUCE, SUCH AS ARUGULA, CILANTRO, OR WATERCRESS. THE ORIGINAL RECIPE CALLS FOR PINE NUTS, BUT OTHER NUTS, INCLUDING HAZELNUTS, WALNUTS, AND PECANS CAN ALSO BE USED.

Place the basil, parsley, garlic, lemon juice, pine nuts, and grated cheese in the bowl of a food processor or blender. Process until the mixture is finely ground, scraping down the sides of the bowl as necessary. With the setting on low to medium speed, gradually add the olive oil, scraping down the sides of the bowl as necessary. Continue blending until the sauce is thickened. Season the sauce to taste with salt and pepper.

HERB-FLAVORED OILS

THE CHEFS AT THE STEPHANIE INN OFTEN USE DROPS OF BRIGHTLY COLORED, FLAVORFUL OILS TO GARNISH THE PLATES. YOU CAN USE PARSLEY, WATERCRESS, BASIL, ARUGULA, OR CHIVES INDIVIDUALLY OR IN COMBINATION TO FLAVOR YOUR OWN OILS. THEY WILL KEEP UP TO ONE WEEK IN A COVERED GLASS JAR IN THE REFRIGERATOR. TO REHEAT OIL, SET THE JAR IN A BOWL OF HOT WATER AND WHISK UNTIL THE OIL SOFTENS.

Trim the herbs from their stems. Place the water and salt in a saucepan and bring the water to a boil. Place the herbs in a strainer and dip them into the boiling water for 1 minute to blanch them, then dip the strainer filled with herbs immediately into a bowl of ice water (to preserve the herb's color). Drain the herbs and pat dry on paper towels. Place the herbs in a blender or food processor with the olive oil and salt. Purée for about 8 minutes, or until the mixture is very smooth and warm (this extracts the color from the herbs).

1   cup chopped herbs, rinsed and patted dry on paper towels

2   cups water

1/8   teaspoon salt

Ice water, as needed

3/4   cup olive oil

Pinch of salt

MAKES ABOUT 1 CUP

APRICOT & APPLE CHUTNEY

1   tablespoon olive oil

2   tablespoons butter

1   small onion, diced

1   cup dried apricots, diced

1   apple, peeled, cored and diced

1   tablespoon mustard seed

1   tablespoon ground cinnamon

1/2 teaspoon ground nutmeg

1/2 teaspoon dry mustard

1/2 teaspoon ground cloves

1/2 teaspoon ground ginger

1/2 cup brown sugar

4   tablespoons cider vinegar

FLAVORED WITH GINGER AND OTHER AROMATIC SPICES, THIS THICK CHUTNEY IS EXCELLENT WITH GRILLED OR ROAST PORK. IT ALSO MAKES A WONDERFUL SAUCE FOR GRILLED FISH, SUCH AS HALIBUT OR SALMON. IT WILL KEEP UP TO 1 WEEK IN THE REFRIGERATOR.

Heat the olive oil and butter in a saucepan over medium-high heat. Stir in the onion, apricots, apple and mustard seed. Stir often, until the onions and apple are tender. (If the mixture becomes dry, add a little water). Stir in the remaining ingredients. Bring the mixture to a boil, and then reduce the heat to a simmer. Cook for about 15 minutes, stirring often to prevent scorching. Serve warm or chilled.

MAKES ABOUT 2 CUPS

THE COOKIE JAR

GUESTS OF THE STEPHANIE INN ARE GREETED WITH A
WARM SMILE FROM THE HOST AT THE FRONT DESK AND A
COOKIE JAR FILLED WITH JUST-BAKED COOKIES. WHEN
GUESTS LEAVE, THEY ARE BID FAREWELL WITH MORE
COOKIES AND OTHER GOODIES. THE POPULAR COOKIE JAR
SITS ON THE FRONT DESK, DAY AND NIGHT, READY TO
PLEASE HUNGRY BEACHCOMBERS.

LEMON-COCONUT BARS
WALNUTS & RAISINS

Preheat the oven to 350° F.

In a mixing bowl, combine the flour and brown sugar. Cut in the butter until it is reduced to small bits and the mixture can be pressed together between your fingers. Lightly grease a 13" x 9½" baking pan. Press the crust into the bottom of the pan and bake it for about 12 minutes or until golden.

In a mixing bowl, whisk together the eggs, sugar and salt. Stir in the remaining ingredients and spread the topping evenly over the hot crust. Return the pan to the oven and bake for about 25 minutes or until the topping is set and lightly browned. Remove from the oven and let cool to room temperature. Slice into individual pieces.

MAKES ABOUT 28 COOKIES

CRUST
2	cups all-purpose flour
1/4	cup brown sugar
1/2	cup (1 stick) butter, softened

TOPPING
3	eggs, beaten
2	cups sugar
1/2	teaspoon salt
1	cup shredded, sweetened coconut
1/2	cup raisins
1/2	cup walnuts, chopped
4	tablespoons fresh lemon juice
2	teaspoons lemon zest

ORANGE COCONUT MACAROONS

Preheat the oven to 350° F.

Grease two baking sheets, or line with parchment paper.

Combine all of the ingredients in a mixing bowl. Mix thoroughly. Drop by spoonfuls onto the prepared baking sheets and bake for 10 to 15 minutes, or until golden.

MAKES ABOUT 24 COOKIES

	Juice of 1 orange
14	ounces shredded, sweetened coconut
14	ounces sweetened condensed milk
2	teaspoons almond extract
1	teaspoon vanilla extract

STEPHANIE INN GINGERSNAPS

1/3 cup butter, softened

1 cup sugar

1 egg

1/3 cup molasses

2 teaspoons white vinegar

3 cups bread flour or all-purpose flour

2 teaspoons baking soda

1/2 teaspoon salt

2 teaspoons powdered cinnamon

2 teaspoons powdered ginger

1/2 teaspoon powdered cardamom

Preheat the oven to 350° F.

Grease two baking sheets.

In a mixing bowl, cream together the butter and sugar at high speed. Reduce the speed to medium; add the egg, molasses and vinegar and mix well. In a separate bowl, combine the flour, baking soda, ginger, cinnamon and cardamom. Gradually add the dry ingredients to the butter mixture, mixing thoroughly.

Using a 2-inch round ice cream scoop, spoon the cookie dough onto greased baking sheets, leaving 2 inches between cookies. Using the palm of your hand, gently press each cookie until it is slightly flattened. Bake the cookies for about 12 minutes, or until they are lightly golden. Let the cookies cool to room temperature before storing.

MAKES ABOUT 24 COOKIES

STEPHANIE INN SNICKERDOODLES

1¾ cups butter, softened

1¾ cups brown sugar

1 cup white sugar

4 eggs

1 tablespoon vanilla extract

4½ cups all-purpose flour

1 teaspoon baking soda

1/2 teaspoon salt

1 cup sugar, mixed with 2 teaspoons cinnamon for topping

Preheat the oven to 350° F.

Grease two baking sheets.

In a mixing bowl, cream the butter and sugar together at high speed, until light and fluffy. Reduce the mixer speed to medium, and add the eggs, one at a time and the vanilla, mixing well. Gradually add the dry ingredients, mixing thoroughly. Using a 2-inch ice cream scoop, spoon the cookie dough onto the greased baking sheets. Flatten each cookie slightly with the palm of your hand, and sprinkle with cinnamon sugar. Bake for about 12 minutes, or until the cookies are golden. Let the cookies cool to room temperature before storing.

MAKES ABOUT 24 COOKIES

CHOCOLATE DECADENCE

SILKY AND RICH, WITH A DIVINE CHOCOLATE FLAVOR, THIS IS DELICIOUS SERVED WITH CARAMEL SAUCE AND WHIPPED CREAM. CANDIED WALNUTS ARE A FAVORITE CHEFS' GARNISH FOR THIS AND OTHER DESSERTS. (SEE RECIPE INDEX FOR CARAMEL SAUCE AND CANDIED WALNUTS RECIPES)

To make the Chocolate Cake: Preheat the oven to 325° F. Line a 9-inch spring-form pan with parchment paper. Grease the parchment and sprinkle it lightly with sugar.

Melt the butter and the chocolate in the top of a double boiler over medium heat, stirring often. Remove the chocolate from the heat and whisk in the egg yolks, one at a time, incorporating well after each addition. Whisk in the vanilla.

In a separate bowl, mix the sugar, salt, and cocoa powder together, then whisk the dry ingredients into the chocolate mixture. Pour the egg whites into a clean mixing bowl and whip until soft peaks are formed. Gently fold the egg whites into the chocolate batter and then turn the mixture into the prepared pan. Bake the mixture for about 40 minutes, or just until the center is firm. Don't worry about cracks around the edges. Let the cake cool in the pan for about 15 minutes. Run a knife around the sides of the pan. Place a plate over the top of the cake and, holding it firmly, invert the cake onto the plate. Remove the pan and remove the parchment paper from the bottom of the cake.

To make the Chocolate Glaze: Place the chopped chocolate and heavy cream in the top of a double boiler over medium heat. Heat, stirring often, until the chocolate is melted and the mixture is smooth and creamy. Pour the warm glaze over the cake and, using a metal spatula, smooth the glaze over the top and around the sides of the cake. Chill the cake until the glaze has set.

To serve: Slice and place on dessert plates. Garnish with Caramel Sauce and Candied Walnuts.

CHOCOLATE CAKE

2   cups (4 sticks) unsalted butter, softened

1   pound bittersweet chocolate, chopped

11 eggs, separated

2   tablespoons vanilla extract

1¾ cups sugar

1/4 teaspoon salt

1/4 cup cocoa powder

CHOCOLATE GLAZE

8   ounces bittersweet chocolate, chopped

6   ounces heavy cream

CARAMEL SAUCE

(see Recipe Index)

CANDIED WALNUTS

(see Recipe Index)

SERVES 12

TART CRUST

1⅓ cups all-purpose flour

1/3 cup brown sugar

1/3 cup ground almonds

1/2 teaspoon nutmeg

1/2 teaspoon lemon zest

2/3 cup unsalted butter, chilled and
cut into 1/2-inch pieces

MASCARPONE CHEESE FILLING

1⅓ cups mascarpone cheese

2/3 cup powdered sugar

Whole fresh strawberries to cover
the filling

1/2 cup apricot or strawberry jam

SERVES 8 TO 10

STRAWBERRY MASCARPONE TART

FRESH OREGON STRAWBERRIES ARE THE ULTIMATE—DEEP RED TO THE CORE AND BURSTING WITH FLAVOR. HERE THEY ARE SET IN A BUTTERY, GROUND ALMOND CRUST WITH A RICH MASCARPONE FILLING.

MASCARPONE IS A THICK, SWEET CHEESE MADE FROM CULTURED FRESH CREAM. IT CAN BE FOUND IN THE CHEESE SECTION OF MOST GROCERY STORES (USUALLY IN PLASTIC TUBS). IF IT IS NOT AVAILABLE, YOU CAN SUBSTITUTE CREAM CHEESE.

To prepare the Tart Crust: Preheat the oven to 350° F. In a food processor, combine the flour, brown sugar, ground almonds, nutmeg, and lemon zest. Add the chilled butter and process until the mixture is crumbly and sticks together when pressed between your fingers. Press the filling into a greased 10-inch tart pan with a removable bottom, spreading the crust over the bottom and up the sides of the pan. Refrigerate or freeze the crust just until it is firm. Remove and bake for about 15 minutes or until golden brown. Remove the crust from the oven and allow it to cool to room temperature.

To make the Mascarpone Cheese Filling: Combine the mascarpone cheese and the powdered sugar in a mixing bowl and whisk until the sugar is incorporated. Add the almond extract and spread the mixture over the bottom of the cooled crust.

To assemble the tart: Wipe the strawberries clean with a damp cloth and remove their stems. Beginning at the outer edge of the tart, set the strawberries, pointed side up, in concentric circles, ending in the center of the tart. Heat the jam in a small saucepan over medium heat. When it is melted, strain it through a sieve. Using a soft pastry brush, brush the tops and sides of the strawberries with the jam. Chill for about 2 hours or until the mascarpone cheese and jam have set.

To serve: Holding the sides of the pan, carefully lift the removable bottom with the tart up and out of the pan. Set the tart on a serving tray and slice into wedges.

GRAHAM CRACKER CRUST

2 cups graham cracker crumbs

1/2 cup sugar

1/2 cup (1 stick) unsalted butter, melted

CREAM CHEESE HUCKLEBERRY FILLING

2½ cups cream cheese, softened

1 cup sugar

1 tablespoon vanilla extract

6 eggs, room temperature

1 cup huckleberries or blueberries

HUCKLEBERRY SAUCE

1½ cups huckleberries

1/2 cup water

1 cup sugar

2 tablespoons cornstarch mixed with

2 tablespoons water

SERVES 12 TO 16

HUCKLEBERRY CHEESECAKE
HUCKLEBERRY SAUCE

WILD BLUE HUCKLEBERRIES FROM THE OREGON COAST ARE THE CHEFS' FAVORITE, BUT BLUEBERRIES MAKE A WONDERFUL SUBSTITUTE. THIS CHEESECAKE NEEDS TO CHILL AT LEAST 4 HOURS BEFORE SERVING. CHILLING OVERNIGHT IS RECOMMENDED.

To make the Graham Cracker Crust: Preheat the oven to 325° F. In a mixing bowl, combine the graham cracker crumbs and sugar. Stir in the melted butter, mixing well. Grease the bottom of a 10-inch spring-form pan. Pour the crust mixture into the pan and use the back of a soup spoon to press it evenly over the bottom of the pan and 1 inch up the sides. Chill the crust until it is firm.

To prepare the Cream Cheese Huckleberry Filling: In a mixing bowl, beat the softened cream cheese at high speed in a mixing bowl until it is smooth and creamy. Reduce the speed and add the sugar, mixing well. Add the eggs, one at a time, scraping down the sides of the bowl as necessary and then add the vanilla. Beat until the ingredients in the mixture are well incorporated. Fold 1 cup of huckleberries into the mixture, and then pour it into the prepared crust. Bake the cheesecake in the preheated oven for about 1 hour and 15 minutes, or until a knife inserted in the center comes out almost clean. Remove the cheesecake from the oven and cool on a wire rack until it is cool enough to handle. Chill the cheesecake at least 4 hours before serving.

To make the Huckleberry Sauce: Combine the huckleberries, sugar, and water in a saucepan over medium-high heat. Bring the mixture to a boil, then reduce the heat to a simmer and cook, stirring often, for about 15 minutes. In a small bowl, mix the cornstarch with 2 tablespoons water. Stir the cornstarch into the huckleberries, stirring constantly until slightly thickened.

To serve: Run a knife around the edges of the spring-form pan to loosen the crust. Remove cheesecake from the pan and slice into 12 to 16 portions. Serve cheesecake on dessert plates and ladle a large spoonful of Huckleberry Sauce over the top of each serving.

WHITE CHOCOLATE CHEESECAKE
DARK CHOCOLATE GLAZE

CREAM CHEESE AND CHOCOLATE—COULD THERE BE A MORE LUXURIOUS COMBINATION? THIS RECIPE TAKES THE ULTIMATE CHEESECAKE ONE STEP BEYOND BY INCLUDING BOTH WHITE AND BITTERSWEET CHOCOLATE.

To make the White Chocolate Cream Cheese Filling: Preheat the oven to 325° F. In a mixing bowl, beat the cream cheese with the sugar until the mixture is smooth and creamy. Add the vanilla and cornstarch, mixing well. Add the eggs and yolks, one at a time, scraping down the sides of the bowl, as necessary. Mix in the half-and-half and the sour cream. Fold in the melted white chocolate. Wrap the bottom of the spring-form pan with aluminum foil and set the pan in a bain marie*. Pour the cream cheese filling into the prepared crust. Fill the bain marie with enough water to come 3 inches up the side of the cheesecake. Place the pan in the preheated oven and bake for about 40 minutes or until a knife inserted in the center comes out clean.

To prepare the Chocolate Glaze: Place the cream in a heavy-bottomed saucepan and bring it to the scalding point over medium-high heat. Reduce the heat to low; add the corn syrup and chopped chocolate, and stir until the chocolate is melted and the mixture is smooth. Remove the pan from the heat and then stir in the liquor and vanilla. Pour the glaze over the warm cheesecake, smoothing it with a spatula. Chill the cheesecake overnight in the refrigerator.

To serve: Run a knife around the edges of the spring-form pan to loosen the crust. Remove the cheesecake from the pan and slice into 12 to 16 portions.

* Bain marie: large baking pan with sides.

GRAHAM CRACKER CRUST
Follow the graham cracker crust recipe in the Huckleberry Cheesecake Recipe (page 142).

WHITE CHOCOLATE CREAM CHEESE FILLING
2½   pounds cream cheese, softened
1¾   cups sugar
2   teaspoons vanilla extract
3   tablespoons cornstarch
5   eggs
2   egg yolks
1/4 cup half-and-half
1/4 cup sour cream
7½   ounces white chocolate, melted

CHOCOLATE GLAZE
1   cup heavy cream
3   tablespoons light corn syrup
7½   ounces bittersweet or semi-sweet chocolate, finely chopped
1   tablespoon Godiva liqueur or Grand Marnier
3/4 teaspoon vanilla

SERVES 12 TO 16

Women of The Stephanie Inn:
Jennifer Booth

Jennifer Anne Schwartz Booth, for whom one of the rooms at The Stephanie Inn is named, was raised in the Midwest. She and her husband, Bill Booth, close friends of Jan Martin and the late Steve Martin, are part owners of The Stephanie Inn. Jennifer moved to Oregon in 1973, and she soon discovered the beauty of the Pacific Ocean and Cannon Beach. Jennifer lives in The Dalles, Oregon, with her husband, Bill. She is the president of Medi-Mech Corporation (a manufacturer of internationally distributed medical equipment). When she is not busy working, or taking care of the family home, she also pursues her interests in art, literature, and photography. Whenever they have a chance, Jennifer and her family visit Cannon Beach and her namesake room, the Jennifer Anne, at The Stephanie Inn.

Jennifer Booth's
Lemon Cake Custard

WONDERFULLY LEMONY AND REFRESHING, THIS DESSERT FROM JENNIFER BOOTH IS SOMETHING BETWEEN A CUSTARD AND A SPONGE CAKE. WITH A DUSTING OF POWDERED SUGAR, A DOLLOP OF SWEETENED WHIPPED CREAM AND A FEW STRANDS OF LEMON ZEST AS THE FINISHING TOUCHES, IT PROVIDES AN ELEGANT AND REFRESHING FINISH TO ANY MEAL.

Preheat the oven to 325° F.

Butter six 1/2-cup-capacity ramekins (or a 1-quart capacity bowl or soufflé dish) and sprinkle the bottoms lightly with sugar.

In a mixing bowl, beat the egg yolks at high speed until thick and lemon-colored, about 3 minutes. Add the sugar and softened butter, mixing well. Add the flour, and then gradually add the milk, scraping down the sides of the bowl as necessary. Mix in the lemon rind and lemon juice.

In a clean mixing bowl, beat the egg whites with the salt until soft peaks form (almost stiff, but still moist and glossy). Using a rubber spatula, fold the beaten egg whites into the yolk mixture, mixing thoroughly. Distribute the mixture among the prepared ramekins. Tap them gently on the counter to level them before placing the ramekins in a large baking pan with sides (bain marie). Fill the pan with warm water 1/2-inch up the sides of the ramekins. Place the pan in the warm oven and bake for about 50 minutes, or until the custards are set, and a knife inserted in the center just comes out clean. Remember that they will continue to cook a little once they are removed from the oven.

Remove the pan from the oven and transfer the lemon custards to a cooling rack.

To serve: Just before serving, sprinkle the custards with powdered sugar, top with a dollop of whipped cream, and add a sprinkle of lemon zest. This dessert may be served warm, at room temperature, or chilled.

3   egg yolks (reserve the whites for later use)

1   cup sugar

2   tablespoons unsalted butter, softened

1/4 cup sifted all-purpose flour

1   cup whole milk

Grated rind of 1 lemon

1/3 cup fresh lemon juice

Reserved egg whites

1/4 teaspoon salt

Powdered sugar, whipped cream, and lemon zest for garnish

SERVES 6

HAZELNUT CRUST

2   cups ground toasted hazelnuts

1/2 cup brown sugar

1/4 teaspoon ground nutmeg

5   tablespoons melted unsalted butter

CHOCOLATE MOUSSE

1   cup (2 sticks) unsalted butter, softened

1   cup sugar

8   eggs

1¼ pounds bittersweet chocolate, melted and slightly cooled

1/4 cup half-and-half

CHOCOLATE GANACHE

7½ ounces bittersweet chocolate, chopped

2/3 cup heavy cream

1   teaspoon unsalted butter

SERVES 12

CHOCOLATE HAZELNUT TORTE

IF YOU ARE LOOKING FOR THE ULTIMATE CHOCOLATE DESSERT, THIS STEPHANIE INN FAVORITE IS A GREAT CHOICE! A TOASTY HAZELNUT CRUST IS FILLED WITH A LUXURIOUSLY RICH CHOCOLATE MOUSSE AND TOPPED WITH A RICH CHOCOLATE GANACHE. (YOU CAN SUBSTITUTE WALNUTS OR PECANS FOR THE HAZELNUTS.) SERVE WITH A DARK-ROAST COFFEE OR, FOR A SPECIAL TREAT, A GLASS OF PORT OR COGNAC. THIS DESSERT WILL KEEP UP TO ONE WEEK IN THE REFRIGERATOR.

Line the bottom of a 9-inch spring-form pan with waxed paper or parchment paper. Grease lightly.

To make the Hazelnut Crust: In a mixing bowl, combine the toasted nuts, brown sugar and nutmeg. Stir in the melted butter. Using the back of a wooden spoon, press the mixture into the bottom of the spring-form pan. Chill until set.

To make the Chocolate Mousse: Whip the softened butter until light and creamy. Whisk in the sugar and then the eggs, one at a time, beating thoroughly after each addition. With the mixer on low speed, add the melted chocolate and half-and-half. Pour over the chilled crust and refrigerate until set.

To make the Chocolate Ganache: Place the chopped chocolate and butter in the top of a double boiler and cook over medium heat, whisking often, until melted. Scald the cream and whisk into the chocolate-butter mixture. Let cool slightly, and then pour over the top of the chilled mousse. Refrigerate until cool.

To un-mold and serve: Run a knife around the edge of the torte and remove the side of the spring-form pan. Slice into serving portions with a hot knife.

CHEF'S TIP

When serving desserts, heat a slicing knife by running it under hot water, or dipping it in a pitcher of hot water. Wipe the knife dry before slicing. Reheat and wipe clean before making each slice.

DESSERT SUSHI

1 cup Japanese medium-grain rice, rinsed and drained

1 cup unsweetened coconut milk

1/2 cup water

1/3 cup sugar

Juice of 1/2 lime

1 8" x 8" square fruit leather

1/4 cup cantaloupe, julienned

1/4 cup strawberries, juliennned

1/4 cup honeydew melon, julienned

Strawberry slices for garnish

CHOCOLATE SAUCE
(see next page)

WRAPPED IN FRUIT LEATHER AND FILLED WITH SWEET COCONUT RICE AND FRESH FRUIT, THESE LITTLE GEMS ARE SLICED JUST LIKE SAVORY SUSHI. THEY LOOK JUST LIKE THE REAL THING BUT THEY'RE SWEET. THE STEPHANIE INN CHEFS MAKE THEIR OWN FRUIT LEATHER USING PURÉED KIWI FRUIT, BUT AT HOME YOU CAN SUBSTITUTE PRE-MADE FRUIT LEATHER.

In a medium saucepan, combine the rice, coconut milk, water, and sugar and mix well. Cover the pan and bring the mixture to a boil, watching closely so that it does not boil over. Reduce the heat to a simmer, cover, and cook for about 20 minutes, or until the rice is tender and slightly sticky. Stir in the lime juice and allow the rice to cool to room temperature.

Lay the fruit leather on a sheet of parchment paper or waxed paper. Spread the rice over the lower half of the fruit leather, about 1/4-inch thick. Distribute the julienned fruit in the center of the rice. Starting at the end of the fruit roll with the rice, roll the mixture into a tight roll. Chill the rolls until firm and then cut into 3/4-inch slices.

To serve: Arrange the slices on dessert plates and garnish with strawberry slices and a drizzle of warm Chocolate Sauce.

SERVES 6

CHOCOLATE SAUCE

Place the chocolate and the cream in the top of a double boiler over medium heat. Whisk together until the chocolate is melted and the sauce is creamy and smooth. Serve warm.

8   ounces bittersweet chocolate, chopped

1   cup heavy cream

MAKES ABOUT 2 CUPS

CARAMEL SAUCE

Combine the sugar and water in a heavy-bottomed saucepan, stirring gently with a wooden spoon to combine. Bring the mixture to a boil over medium-high heat and continue boiling until the syrup caramelizes to a golden color, shaking the pan occasionally. Watch the syrup carefully as it can overcook quickly. Remove it from the heat as soon as it caramelizes.

Heat the cream and butter together in a separate saucepan. Gradually whisk the hot cream into the caramelized sugar, and then whisk in the vanilla. If necessary, return the sauce to the heat and whisk until smooth. Serve warm.

1½ cups sugar

1/2 cup cold water

3   tablespoons unsalted butter

1   cup heavy cream

1/2 teaspoon vanilla

MAKES ABOUT 2 CUPS

WHITE & DARK CHOCOLATE TRUFFLES

WHITE CHOCOLATE TRUFFLES

1   pound plus 2-ounces white chocolate, finely chopped

1/2   cup heavy cream

1   tablespoon liqueur, such as Crème de Cocoa or Cognac

DARK CHOCOLATE TRUFFLES

1   pound bittersweet chocolate, finely chopped

1½   cups heavy cream

2   tablespoons liqueur, such as Cognac or Grand Marnier

Cocoa powder, powdered sugar or ground nuts

GUESTS AT THE STEPHANIE INN ARE OFTEN TREATED TO A DESSERT FEATURING BOTH WHITE AND DARK CHOCOLATE TRUFFLES ON THE SIDE. AT HOME, YOU CAN PREPARE ONE OR BOTH VARIETIES, AND THEY DON'T NECESSARILY NEED TO ACCOMPANY A DESSERT. THEY ARE A WONDERFUL TREAT ON THEIR OWN. ALWAYS WARM THE TRUFFLES TO ROOM TEMPERATURE BEFORE SERVING. THEY CAN BE PREPARED UP TO 1 WEEK IN ADVANCE AND ARE SURE TO PLEASE ANY CHOCOLATE LOVER. LOOK FOR QUALITY CHOCOLATE, SUCH AS CALLEBAUT, VAHLRONA, OR GHIRARDELLI.

To make either the White or the Dark Chocolate Truffles, place the chocolate of choice in a stainless steel bowl. Place the heavy cream in a saucepan and bring to a boil over medium-high heat. Pour the hot cream over the chocolate, and let it sit for about 1 minute. Using a wire whisk, stir the mixture until the chocolate is thoroughly melted. Whisk in the liqueur and pour the mixture into a 9- x 11-inch baking pan.

Place the truffle mixture in the refrigerator until it is thoroughly chilled, at least 3 hours.

When the chocolate mixture is firm, remove it from the refrigerator and, using a teaspoon or melon baller, scoop the truffles into rounds. Roll the mixture in your hands to form little balls. Roll the truffles in cocoa powder, powdered sugar, or ground nuts, and let sit at room temperature until serving time.

MAKES ABOUT
16 TRUFFLES EACH

CANDIED WALNUTS

SERVE THESE ADDICTIVELY DELICIOUS CANDIED WALNUTS AS A GARNISH FOR DESSERTS, OR AS A SNACK WITH YOUR FAVORITE COCKTAIL. THEY ARE ALSO THE PERFECT GARNISH FOR THE STEPHANIE INN'S CHOCOLATE DECADENCE (SEE RECIPE INDEX).

1   pound walnut halves

1¼ cups sugar, divided

3/4 cup water

1/2 teaspoon kosher salt

Preheat the oven to 350° F.

Spread the walnuts on a baking sheet and bake for about 10 minutes, or until golden. Meanwhile, place the water and 3/4 cup of the sugar in a heavy-bottomed saucepan over high heat. Bring the mixture to a boil. Reduce the heat to a simmer and cook for about 20 minutes or until the syrup is golden and lightly caramelized. Place the toasted walnuts in a large mixing bowl and pour the hot syrup over the walnuts, mixing thoroughly. Using a slotted spoon, remove the walnuts from the syrup and place them on a clean, lightly greased baking sheet. Return the walnuts to the oven and bake for about 5 minutes, or until they are dry. Sprinkle the remaining 1/2 cup sugar and the kosher salt over the walnuts, and toss to coat the walnuts on all sides. Allow the walnuts to cool to room temperature before storing in airtight containers. These will keep up to one week.

MAKES 1 POUND

recipe index

index

STEVE MARTIN (1943-2000)

Stephanie (left), Jan (right), and Steve Martin (front center)

STEVE MARTIN AND HIS WIFE, JANICE KAY MARTIN, BECAME HOTELIERS WITH THE PURCHASE OF THE SURFSAND RESORT IN 1979, FOLLOWED BY THE PURCHASE OF THE VIKING MOTEL, THE HAYSTACK RESORT, THE WAYFARER RESTAURANT, AND THE RV RESORT—ALL IN CANNON BEACH. THEY ALSO OWNED THE QUALITY INN AND COUSINS RESTAURANT IN THE DALLES, OREGON. IN 1993, THEY BUILT THE STEPHANIE INN IN THE SHADOW OF THE OLD VIKING MOTEL. STEVE WAS ALSO THE CEO OF STEVE MARTIN MANAGEMENT COMPANY, WHERE HE EARNED THE DESIGNATION OF "SMALL BUSINESS MAN OF THE YEAR" IN 1988.

STEVE'S MOTTO WAS "THE CUSTOMER IS ALWAYS RIGHT." ALL WHO KNEW HIM RECOGNIZED HIS PASSION FOR HIS GUESTS AND HIS LOVE FOR HIS EMPLOYEES. HE LIKED TO DO THINGS DIFFERENTLY AND THE STEPHANIE INN IS A PERFECT EXAMPLE. HE INSTILLED IN ALL AT THE INN THE IMPORTANCE OF OFFERING EXCELLENT CUSTOMER SERVICE, HELPING GUESTS CREATE GREAT MEMORIES AND ALWAYS DOING SO WITH AN ENTHUSIASTIC SMILE.

NOT ONLY WAS STEVE KNOWN AS AN ENTREPRENEUR AND A GOOD BUSINESSMAN, HE WILL ALSO BE LONG REMEMBERED FOR HIS KIND AND HELPFUL NATURE. HE LOVED CANNON BEACH AND THE PEOPLE THERE. WHETHER IT WAS AN EMPLOYEE DOWN ON HIS LUCK, A FRIEND IN NEED, OR SOMEONE WHO JUST NEEDED HIS EXPERTISE IN BUSINESS, HE WAS ALWAYS READY TO LISTEN AND HELP IN ANY WAY HE COULD. SEEING OTHERS ACCOMPLISH THEIR GOALS WAS STEVE MARTIN'S GREATEST REWARD.

STEVE MARTIN PASSED AWAY ON AUGUST 11, 2000, AFTER A THREE-YEAR BATTLE WITH CANCER. HE WAS LOVED AND RESPECTED BY MANY AND IS SORELY MISSED.